The 12 Truths*
About Surviving
and Succeeding
in the Office

*And Some of Them
Aren't Very Nice

The 12 Truths*
About Surviving
and Succeeding
in the Office

*And Some of Them
Aren't Very Nice

Karen Randall

B

BERKLEY BOOKS, NEW YORK

This is an original publication of The Berkley Publishing Group.

THE TWELVE TRUTHS* ABOUT SURVIVING AND
SUCCEEDING IN THE OFFICE
*and some of them aren't very nice

A Berkley Book / published by arrangement with
the author

PRINTING HISTORY
Berkley trade paperback edition / May 1997

The Putnam Berkley World Wide Web site address is
http://www.berkley.com

ISBN: 0-425-15621-4

BERKLEY®
Berkley Books are published by The Berkley Publishing Group,
200 Madison Avenue, New York, New York 10016.
BERKLEY and the "B" design
are trademarks belonging to Berkley Publishing Corporation.

PRINTED IN THE UNITED STATES OF AMERICA

10 9 8 7 6 5 4 3 2 1

Acknowledgments

Many thanks to my editor, Hillary Cige, and my editor-in-chief, Leslie Gelbman, for giving me this opportunity. Also, much appreciation for my brilliant agent, Denise Stinson.

Without the friendship and encouragement from the following people, this past year and the writing of this book would have been difficult: Mauro di Preta, Diane Goldner, the Kelly family, Larry Kirshbaum, Walter Leib, Bobbi Mark, Colleen Murphy, Patty Powers, Gil Schwartz, Al Silverman, Ganga Stone, and Brigitte Weeks.

But my most special thanks goes to my dear and precious friend, Charles Winecoff—his help, encouragement, support, and faith in me cannot be quantified. Thank you.

—February 1996

To my beloved husband, Randy Sandke.
Someone to watch over me . . .

A Note About This Book

*E*ach of The 12 Truths has its own chapter. Sometimes you'll see expressions or words in bold type. These are terms that have a unique meaning (that I made up, in most cases). In case they don't make immediate sense to you, you'll find the meanings in the back of the book, in the glossary.

The 12 Truths

The 12 Truths*
About Surviving
and Succeeding
in the Office

*And Some of Them
Aren't Very Nice

Introduction

There are two kinds of offices: those that run on pathology, jealousy, anger, and nastiness; and those that are much more sane and compassionate. This book tells you how to work in and deal with the first kind, which is, unfortunately, also the most common. You don't need to take a quiz to find out which kind of office you work in; you should have been able to figure it out during your first week on the job.

Taking that into account, you are about to read a book like no other office self-help book. *The 12 Truths* is unique in that it deals with office survival in a straightforward, honest, no-bullshit way. Most office self-help books offer advice that starts with, "Be nice and polite to everyone, work hard, turn the other cheek, and everything will go your way." We all know from seeing many incompetents in highly paid positions in all kinds of organizations that this idea is completely false. The fact is, you don't have to be brilliant, funny, nice, or sane to be successful in an office.

I learned the 12 truths a long time ago. At the time, I couldn't believe my intuition about offices. I was, after all, somewhat new to the workplace. I would tell myself that my feelings were mean, or they meant I was bitter, or that I lacked compassion.

Of course, like many of us, I was simply afraid of the truth. I didn't want to believe that office realities are not always blue skies and happy endings. I didn't want to admit that protecting myself and my career were more important than being nice to other people.

I didn't want to face up to the fact that the workplace dynamic is *not* like your family or a marriage or a team (concepts many employers like to perpetuate ad nauseam because it makes it easier for them to manipulate us). Work is a place where we make a living, do something interesting, and develop and maintain our healthy ego and self-esteem. Or it should be. Those are *really* terrific reasons to work. And guess what? They're the *only* reasons to work.

One day, I had the quintessential breakthrough experience when I realized that everything I had felt, but was afraid to admit and put into practice, was true. I was fired. The circumstances seemed unusual, but they weren't. It wasn't, "You're doing a lousy job, you're out." In fact, I was doing a great job, which made it even worse. But that didn't matter; it often doesn't. Because of many difficult things that happened in succession over a short period of time, I lost my center. I was overwhelmed, and I forgot about the *truths*. That was my real downfall.

Many factors come into play when someone is fired: power struggles, broken promises, jealousy, harassment, idle gossip, backstabbing—all part of business as usual. Sometimes people get fired because things aren't going well, and the company just wants a change. Or it could be because a person with some say just decides she doesn't want you around anymore. Performance has nothing to do with it—it rarely does. If that were the case, half the people you work with would be unemployed.

Getting fired, negotiating my way through that process—thinking about what I had and hadn't done in that particular job, looking back at how I had interacted with my colleagues—was a great gift. It made me see, at last, that I had been right all along. I should have paid attention to the voice inside me; I got fired because I ignored it. Mostly, I shouldn't have ever bothered trying to cooperate with or understand these particular people. That just made me crazy. As soon as I realized how manipulative and detrimental they could be, I should have simply protected myself from them instead of trying to fit in.

Supportive friends who encouraged and comforted me were a reminder of what real friends and compassionate human beings are, and they proved that understanding and patience is sometimes even more helpful than getting a tip about a job possibility or an offer of good advice at the worst possible moment. I value people who realize and acknowledge that *yes*, people in offices can have serious problems—it's not all your fault if things go wrong. That's why now whenever someone asks for help getting a job, polishing a resumé, getting through a tough period at work, or negotiating a raise or settlement, I am not only happy—but committed—to helping them out. I guess it's the real reason I wrote this book—to help people I may never meet.

However, I owe more thanks to all the dreadful, nasty, psychopathic, and troubled people I have worked with than I do to the kind and nurturing ones. The bad ones have taught me the most about myself and what it takes to sit in an office all day and try to do something interesting without losing my mind.

This is not to say that the 12 truths will keep you from being fired. Conventional business wisdom says that every person will be fired or laid off an average of three times in his or her working lifetime. However, the 12 truths will keep propelling you forward and help keep your self-esteem intact. And if you *are* fired, they will help you even then by showing you how to be **Fired Smart**.

I hope some of the 12 truths make you laugh. I know some of them will make you cringe, a sure sign of recognition. I hope some of them make you angry enough to motivate you to change. Because that's what truth does. If it doesn't happen, then I've failed. I don't want anyone reading this book ever to make the mistake of screwing up at work because they didn't go in with the full knowledge of what offices are like. Or, worse, to not get the most out of each workday and thrive to tell the tale.

The 12 Truths isn't about stabbing people in the back, being nasty, cheating, or stealing (although plenty of people in offices spend their careers doing those things). It's about being strong at work, knowing what to focus on, and what (and who) you need

to forget about. The truths that follow will help gal-
vanize you for all the things that can happen in the
office so you can weather them successfully. I hope
they will teach you that you can never expect or pre-
pare for a specific outcome, but that you can be ready
for *any* situation.

The 12 Truths can't explain why there are mon-
strous people in your office, and I'm certainly not
recommending that you become one. I want this
book to help you recognize the hypocrisy and dis-
honesty in your office (two major management prac-
tices) and deal with them effectively. You can make
every truth here work for you without sacrificing civ-
ilized, dignified behavior, even if others in your office
already have.

This book is based on fifteen years of personal
experience, and the experiences of others who were
in the same boat I was. They're also based on my
years observing people who had terrific, high-paying,
executive jobs, but were not extraordinarily intelligent, appealing, or competent.

I used to wonder, as many of you have, I'm sure,
"How can Joe be a vice president, making $350,000
a year? He can't make a decision, he treats underlings
like crap, and many ideas he's put through have
failed and lost the company money. But he keeps on

going!" Well, I think this guy should be canned, too, but he never will be. He might even get a promotion. Why? Because he instinctively knows some version of the twelve truths and he uses them every day.

You don't have to be super-talented or wildly creative to do well at work. Most people aren't geniuses. Successful people are more shrewd than smart; they think only about themselves and never think about their colleagues—except when someone gets in their way (and then they quickly dispense with the offender).

You have a choice. Many people who have climbed to the top have lost a lot of things along the way: friends, marriages, happiness, health, compassion, their souls. Look around your office at the people who have the best job titles and make the most money (two bourgeois notions of success in American business) and you'll get a pretty clear idea of what it will take out of you to be successful there. Is there anyone in that office you'd trade places with? Is there anyone's life you'd like to be leading? Do the people look happy? Do they look sour? Are they healthy looking? Are they overweight or physically run-down? Do they have clear skin and bright eyes? Do they have troubling addictions to food or cigarettes or alcohol? Do they have happy relationships and marriages? Really look and think about it. The answers to those questions will give you a good indication of how to flourish there. Some offices run on the pathology and the personal misery of their employees; others don't. Decide what kind of office suits you before putting the effort into making this book work for you. Just because a company is financially successful does not guarantee that its employees are happy and kind *or that it's a good place for you to work.*

It seems to me that many of the books published about office politics are written by people who haven't spent much time in real offices. Often, the authors are business psychologists, human resource professionals, professors of business science or CEOs of companies—individuals who are generally surrounded by yes people. They haven't had to deal with a bunch of dysfunctional, unhappy, craven middle managers, so how do they know what to say to you? The 12 truths don't come from a famous psychologist or spiritual leader. They don't come from a professor at Harvard Business School. They come from me, a worker like you. Nothing fancy.

I have purposely made this book short and to the point. I haven't bothered with psychobabble or businesspeak because I don't know any, and you don't need it. I want you to be able to read this book a couple of times and memorize the points. I want you to be able to refer to it for inspiration when things aren't going right, and you think you're falling back on your old work self.

Essential Ingredients for Strength and Success at Work

Getting rid of fear

Fear holds people back. Never be scared of saying what you think or asking for what you need. Don't be afraid of the people around you.

Detaching from your job

This means doing your job, being excited about your job, but not forming an emotional attachment to it. Then, when bad things happen, you'll be able to cope.

Working for yourself

I don't necessarily mean starting your own business. It's doing what you like to do in a way that will help *you* get ahead or attain a specific goal. Good for the company; *great* for you.

Confronting problems when you have them

Don't complain—*act*. If something is bothering you, do something about it.

Not allowing work to become your life

Have other interests. Combining work time with personal time as your main source of social contact is a really bad idea. When an executive tells you, as one once told me, that blending social life with professional life was the only way to do good business— and she didn't mean forming friendly relationships with people in the same business over lunch or a drink, she meant that your weekend and evening activities should be full of people from your business—I recommend steering clear of such a situation. Needless to say, she was lonely and unhappy. Oh, but she had a high salary and did very little, so I guess she felt it was worth it for her.

Controlling your own destiny

Never give anyone power over your job, your future, your goals. Make career decisions based on what you want, not on what your boss wants. You should please your boss, and he does have a certain amount of control over your job growth, but always keep *your* personal goal in mind and work for that, too.

Being yourself
Know who you are and have a strong sense of identity. Develop it, be it. Don't let anyone intimidate you out of being yourself. There was a terrific article in *Fortune* magazine sometime back, which was about successful women (in this case). Every single one of them said that they never sublimated their femininity (do men ever sublimate their masculinity?) and they always went their own way and gave their customers (or bosses) results while remaining strong and true to themselves and their feminine side. Although many of them were criticized by their "teammates" as too pushy (a code word for original) and some were accused of sleeping with the boss (naturally, if you don't hide behind frumpy outfits and down-at-the-heel shoes, and aren't afraid of being a whole person they'll accuse you of *that*) they all prevailed and became leaders in their fields. Don't hide yourself! If someone doesn't appreciate your qualities, find someone who does.

We're moving into a spiritual time right now, and we hear a lot of talk about global love, forgiveness, and understanding. Being in control of your job and making sure you are treated fairly does not contradict those ideas. An office is a unique environment. You can and should maintain a spiritual well-being at the office, but you also have to remember that God wants us to have all the things we need to survive; He wants us to do well and to protect ourselves from those who want to deceive us or do us wrong. He is forgiving, so when you make a mistake, don't worry and move on.

Offices in America will always be driven by profit and productivity. Money will always be the central issue in any business, no matter what nicety-nice stuff the boss spouts about "family," "team," and "caring." And that will always motivate an underlying anxiety that comes down from the top.

Combine that with all the family, emotional, spiritual, and physical baggage that all employees bring with them from home, and you'll quickly realize that offices will never be warm and cozy environments. The kinder, gentler approach is never going to get you anywhere at work. *but* . . .

. . . *this stuff does not apply to your personal life!* It doesn't apply to your relationships or friendships. *Love* your mate or spouse. *Cherish* your friends. *Honor* your family. *Pray* to whoever or whatever. *Be kind* to children and animals. *Respect* your neighbors. Keep your community clean. *Just don't confuse any of that with the people at work!*

Good luck!

Say Whatever You Want to Whomever You Want. Just Say It Right.

*T*his may come as a shock to you, but tone of voice loses more arguments than logic or reasoning. Your voice can make or break you at work. It's that simple and that complex. Your voice, used properly, can accomplish a number of useful things. It can calm someone down or excite them. It can get you a date, a raise, a good work assignment, attention, and respect.

First impressions of people are generally based on two things: appearance and voice. Secondary things like smell count, too, but not as much, unless you haven't bathed in a week. That's why it's important to have a strong, clear voice that gives no indication of insecurity, fear, or nervousness, even if you may be feeling those things.

When you learn to modulate your voice, you can control your emotions and not give your real feelings away. Giving your real feelings away at work is a big no-no for the simple, sad-but-true reason that co-workers will seize any opportunity they can to use your emotions against you.

Sometimes, of course, you'll want to show emotion. For example, if you're pitching a new idea, you want your enthusiasm to come through via your facial expressions and your speech—but not to the point that you sound like a zealot. Knowing how to measure passion, anger, concern, and other feelings is essential in getting what you need out of other people. By learning to modulate your voice and focusing on its essence of calm, you can show emotions when and in the fashion *you* want to; not when your heart wants to.

When you're asking for a raise, giving orders, or confronting a colleague about a serious matter, you want a calm, steady sound. Not only does it make you impossible to read, it also makes you disarming. A modulated voice is taken more seriously than almost anything else. In the animal kingdom, stance and eye contact rule. We can use those things, too, but our voice is uniquely powerful. Master it.

If you can't afford a speech class, tape record yourself. Get a friend to help coach you. Listen to yourself over and over again until you get used to the sound of your voice. Say every outrageous thing you can think of as if you were saying "Hello" or "Have a nice day" to a stranger in a shop or on the telephone.

Say, "You are the biggest asshole I've ever met in my life," or "I can't believe how fat your thighs look in that hideous dress" or even "God, you smell like a sulfur factory, don't you ever take a bath?" in the most calm, sincere, emotionless voice possible. Okay, so you'll laugh a few times. The point is to practice saying things that ordinarily may take on an angry, sarcastic, or nasty tone in a perfectly ordinary way.

Being able to say highly charged things without getting upset or showing your feelings gives you a tremendous advantage over your colleagues. Feelings have no place at work. Never have, never will. If you *do* develop any feelings at work, a trained voice can mask them—otherwise you'll have to quit. That was the hardest, and the saddest, lesson I learned. But the chairman of a very successful company once told me that having feelings for people, or expressing them, was one of the worst career mistakes I could make. He was a good example of how successful you could be by repressing spontaneous emotion.

Once you've mastered voice modulation, it will be so much easier to ask anyone at work for whatever you want. It will be simple to tell someone that you don't appreciate something she's done. It will be easier to ask for help. You'll be more convincing when you have to make a case for yourself. In fact, you can say pretty much anything you want to anyone you want if you use the right words with the right tone of voice. Almost any thought or opinion can come out of a person who owns a calm and confident voice.

Don't whine, don't nag, don't harp. Most things should be stated as if you were a newscaster. Be careful not to sound like a robot. You want to sound like you. This is really hard and will require practice. But guess what? It's worth the time. Do it.

TECHNIQUE

My husband is a musician and a composer, so he knows a lot about sound from both a technical and emotional point of view. He's currently doing a very brave and dangerous thing: he's teaching me to sing. Because of this, and because I've been listening to how people sound when they talk all my life, I have now learned quite a bit about talking right.

If you don't like what you hear when you play back your voice on a tape recorder, you must listen very carefully to identify the things that bother you: Is your voice too high, too low, too loud, too soft, high-pitched, nasal, whiny, garbled, uneven, gravelly, marred by a lisp, slowed by a stutter? Only by identifying specifically what you don't like can you hope to correct it. Everyone can fix voice flaws with practice, just like everyone can learn to sing.

Here are some things you can do to improve your voice:

Learn to sing

Even just for fun, singing will teach you a lot about balance, pitch, and control. These components can be transferred to your speaking voice. Acting classes can help, too, because they will train you to pretend, so that if you're upset with a colleague, you can act your way through it and remain calm.

Practice deep breathing

This is helpful in establishing control of tone, pitch, and loudness. Do what your aerobics instructor tells you to do: Breathe deeply in through your nose, and out through your mouth, slowly, from the diaphragm.

Practice good posture

This will enable you to control your voice and project it outward, even if it's soft. In addition, the body language posture conveys is very important and pregnant with meaning. If you're slouching when you talk, you will appear weak; if you fidget, people will think you're lying or evading their questions. Slouching also restricts your breathing and blood flow, hindering your ability to project. To practice good posture, stand against a wall and make sure your shoulders and buttocks are touching the wall. Now, put your arm into the space between your lower back and the wall. Is your hand touching both the wall and your back? If it isn't, tilt your hips so that it does and hold this position for thirty seconds. Repeat.

Chant

You don't have to go to an ashram, and it doesn't have to be loud. Chanting, like deep breathing, centers and calms you, giving you more control over your voice, especially when you are going into an emotionally fraught situation and you have to remain steady. What should you chant? A word or phrase that you like, particularly one conveying strength and energy. "I am powerful." "No one can hurt me." "I will prevail." These, or variations of them, are all excellent choices. Breathe in while you chant the first part of the phrase, breathe out during the second part. If you're using one word only, say it twice, once on the in breath, once on the out.

Vary your voice

Once you feel you have improved your voice and you like it, start to vary it to suit different occasions. Try conveying different emotions through your voice: compassion, sympathy, firm anger, giving orders, flirting, etc. Record yourself and listen with a trusted friend to hear whether you're conveying the emotions you intend.

DO'S AND DON'TS IN SPEAKING

Don't

> *Apologize*—unless you really screwed up; it puts you in a vulnerable position. It's better to "take responsibility" for your mistakes as opposed to saying "sorry."
>
> *Accuse*—it puts people on the defensive, and that can have negative consequences for you. Plus, it's obnoxious.
>
> *Insult*—again, it puts people on the defense, and it puts them off you. Unless you're willing to burn a bridge, hold back slurs.
>
> *Embarrass*—some people in your office love doing this, but I think it's unwise and can put you on the receiving end for the same thing down the road. In any case, it's not really

necessary—most of the people you'd like to embarrass will eventually do it to themselves.

Ask for "favors"—"Can you do me a really big favor?" sounds so smarmy and self-seeking. It's quite flattering and certainly less grabby to ask for a person's expertise or advice.

Look away from the person you're speaking to—it makes them think you wish you weren't there or are actually thinking about the 50%-off sale at Saks.

Repeat yourself—simply boring.

Do

Ask others their opinion (even if you don't care)—it's respectful and makes a lasting, positive impression.

Ask others for their special help—it's flattering, therefore makes for willing assistance.

Be direct—people like it when you get to the point and refrain from long prefaces to get to what you really want.

Keep it short—people appreciate it when you don't waste their time, since most people probably do.

Compliment—not like Eddie Haskell; if you can praise with sincerity, do it; otherwise forget it—it will be completely transparent.

Smile—when appropriate. You don't have to be the court jester, but a pleasant and serene expression can earn you a lot of points—even if they are unconsciously bestowed.

Look at whomever you're addressing—shifty or downcast eyes have always made people uneasy or suspicious.

Overused words to be avoided at all costs

Fabulous—exactly what does this word mean?

Terrific—see above.

Love (as in "You're fabulous! I love you!")—no, you don't. You may love your cat or your mother, but you don't love the deadbeat sitting in the next office.

Incredible and Unbelievable—look them up in the dictionary. Nothing, and I mean nothing, that ever happens at work (unless it's the World Trade Center bombing) merits these expressions.

Nice—huh? "That's nice." "He's nice." Boring, meaningless and inaccurate 90 percent of the time.

Hope (as in you "hope" the person will call you, meet you, give you a raise, etc.)—at the very least this is a stagnant, passive word. Why not say, "I'd like you to . . ." or "I'd appreciate if you could . . ." It's active, shows self-respect, and puts you on equal footing with the person you're approaching.

Other tips for communicating with your colleagues or your superiors

This applies to memos as well as verbal communication.

1. Limit yourself to one or two points at a time.

2. Stick to your points; elaborate just enough for clarity. Don't let yourself get off the subject.

3. Don't boast.

4. Keep your tone even and businesslike. If it shifts, people will sense danger or vulnerability, and they'll go for the jugular. They may also dismiss what you're saying as emotional rather than reasonable.

5. Practice in front of a mirror in advance of any meeting, even if it's with just one other person.

6. Before you go into a meeting, do your deep breathing or chanting exercise. Or take a walk. The goal is to go in feeling calm.

7. Most important of all, don't be afraid to express what you think and want. Only by overcoming any anxiety you may have about saying certain things to particular people will voice modulation work.

Voice modulation is an essential truth. Master it before you put anything else in this book to work.

"The People Make This Place Special!" But You Don't Have to Be Talented, Intelligent, Beautiful, or Even Sane to Be Successful Here.

You hear the first part of this statement from management so often it's become a cliché. But you'll never hear the second half, at least not publicly, even though it's the essential qualifier of the initial statement. You see, there are only two things you must be to get ahead or rest comfortably in your office job: *be* able to satisfy your boss and *be* able to protect yourself. Sounds simple enough, but there can be complications.

For example, beware of allowing yourself to like your coworkers too much. You might start to care what they think, and this could interfere with your quest to please your boss. Trying to please everyone and make them like you is impossible. It's the most basic and important hazard to be avoided. You want your boss—or the person really in charge—to like you. One way of operating is to teach yourself not to care about what Mary in the next office thinks of you. You also become vulnerable to other people if you care about them, and this can give other, less nice types (to be expounded on later) an opportunity to manipulate you, or worse, treat you badly and generally interfere with your goals. That's not protecting yourself. It's why the most successful people in your office are also often the least liked. It's not that coworkers are jealous of their success; they dislike them because nine times out of ten, successful people aren't worried about who likes them, which makes them harder to like.

Many successful office workers have made the decision not to care if they are unpopular or despised. They have purposely lost part of what makes them human—at least when they're at work. This fact doesn't bother the boss. A CEO once said to me, "I don't care how Jack treats his staff or colleagues. He does his job. I don't have time to intervene, and I don't have time to listen to both sides of the story. As long as Jack's performing, he can behave any way he wants to. I'll always go with his side of the story; it's really the only side I want to hear about. It makes my life easier." So much for team spirit.

Aside from making your boss happy and protecting your job, try coming up with one great idea to either make or save your company money. Then you can pretty much rest on your laurels for quite a while. Showing the higher-ups that you're always looking out for the greater good of the company will make a lasting impression. You can continue to get promotions and raises based on that *one* good idea for a fairly long time. Even subsequent mistakes you'll make will be more easily forgotten. Not that coming up with a sensational idea is easy, but the payoff is worth it in terms of advancing your career and a lot of it is the luck of the draw.

That's the key; your boss doesn't have the time to think or care about how his subordinates are treating coworkers. For many of us, it's hard not to care about others, but plenty of people operate that way. They may look miserable, and they probably are miserable, but damn it, they make a good living!

It's easier for the boss to support someone who's leaving him alone and not coming to him with too many problems, even if that person could be doing his job a little better or be a little more talented. Compared to all the other problems a boss may face, someone who is happy with the status quo might be looked on favorably, if only for not being yet another problem. The boss may not even like his employee personally, but he doesn't dislike him. It's difficult to find extraordinarily skillful people (there aren't all that many of them), so bosses will talk themselves into believing that their staff of loyal followers is the best in the business, even if they're not. Unless you're a total moron who starts costing the company money and/or productivity, you don't have to worry about being fired—but you may have to worry about what you'll do next when you succeed!

Of course, there are offices that do care about how employees treat each other, but I believe that those places are the exception, not the rule. Even in a benign office, you don't have to be dazzling to succeed. Average people run businesses—and the country.

However, there are certain kinds of people who thrive in neurotic offices. Their particular brand of mania makes them especially suited for successful office work. So I'd like to spend a few moments talking about these types. The better you know them, the more capable you'll be of handling them. I have not included the ass-kisser as one of the breed because I actually think detaching yourself from the team and setting out to make your boss happy implies that you are one. I guarantee you will come across each and every one of these types in positions more powerful than yours, in every job you have.

The one thing these types have in common is not their ability, expertise, or competency, but the fact that they all make their bosses happy and they know how to protect their turf, despite their different brands of craziness.

When you first start working in a company, everyone seems so nice—warm, generous, helpful. It's not long before the picture becomes clearer, and you begin to see things as they really are.

SCENARIO ONE

"I love my office, Clover. It even has a window! I'm so glad to be here."

"We think you'll like it here, Alice. Everyone works really hard, and we all get along."

Alice likes all her coworkers. They all seem helpful and friendly—showing her where the coffee machine is, the copy machine, the ladies' room. Clover is serious as a manager, but she's straightforward and honest. Alice's first week goes smoothly. She's beginning to understand office procedure, and she's completed her first assignments. She can't wait to hear Clover's response.

Another week passes. Clover comes into Alice's office with her assignments. "You're going to have to do these over, Alice. They're not quite right."

"Oh? I'm sorry. Were there problems with them?"

"Well, I've made some comments. You can go over them when I leave. I won't always be able to guide you this way. Eventually, you'll have to figure out what's wrong with your work on your own," Clover tells Alice. Then she adds with a sarcastic snigger, "But that shouldn't be a problem for you. You're a college graduate."

Alice is stunned. Betsy, Alice's office neighbor, comes in. "I couldn't help overhearing. You got the college graduate routine. Get used to it, and don't think about asking her for help. If you do, she'll never give you a raise."

Bitter Bob or Betty

What drives a person to become resentful and incorporate it into their personal work or management style? Most people who carry that trait as their motivating force believe that they were not given a fair shake in life. They perceive that others think they're inferior, and they fight this perception (which is usually false but can become true, thanks to their own demeanor) with shrewish, dictatorial behavior. They rarely let the people they manage feel accomplished or deserving.

Clover is a **Bitter Betty.** She has worked for the same company all her employable life. She started right out of high school as a clerk in the accounting department of a film company. She was diligent, and her work ethic was fierce. Eventually, Clover got transferred to the sales and marketing department as a junior staff member, correcting copy, filing, and doing routine clerical tasks. Clover made up her mind that she was going to run that department some day, and maybe even the entire company—partly because she enjoyed the business and partly because she hated her boss, whom she considered a snob. She felt the boss scorned her because she'd never gone to college like everyone else in the department had. She worried he would hold her back because he thought she was blue collar and shouldn't be working in something as classy as a film company.

This wasn't true of Clover's boss at all. It *was* true that he was a snob, so actually his condescension was pretty evenly spread around. But deep down, Clover was insecure. She hated people who had gone to college while she'd had to work to help support her family. She hated all the young women in the department who were single and seemed to be out having a good time. She had a baby to take care of and a husband who made a good living but was too tired to help out much at home. But trying to figure all this out on your own is a waste of time. In the first place, you'll never get it right and in the second place your time will be better spent maneuvering around Clover and getting the job done so you can move on.

Clover Spite eventually succeeded in her goal. The snobby boss moved on to another job, and Clover was slowly promoted up through the ranks, until she knew the business inside out, and convinced her new boss, Estelle, to make her the head of the department. She despised the intellectuals and the creative people in the film company to the extent that she made rules barring them from seeing anything she was doing, even if it involved their projects. Estelle indulged her behavior because Clover did her job and didn't complain. As far as Estelle was concerned, Ms. Spite could treat her colleagues and employees any way she wanted to. Clover was particularly tough on the young women in her department, going out of her way not to praise their good work, but she never missed an opportunity to criticize them when they did something wrong. Since she wasn't giving out too many raises, her boss thought the economy of the department was terrific. The fact that her employees and colleagues disliked her and that morale in her department was low made no difference.

A person like Clover may be great for the boss, but she will be difficult for you to work for and with. However, resentful people can often be fooled, and if you are stuck working for them, or if you need to get information from them, you must learn how to ingratiate yourself with them, as this is often the only thing they will respond to.

Let Clover know, subtly, that you feel and understand her resentment. Never act too smart, dress too well, or display any of the symbols of wealth, education, or breeding that she so envies in other people. If you work for her, you should be aware of her opinions and tendencies and make them work for you. Be low key. She doesn't like show-offs. Notice who Clover chooses to associate with in the office. Observe carefully how they interact with her. Do the same. Clover will feel that you're one of her kind and will accept you into the fold.

It seems ridiculous to have to change, perhaps

dramatically, and I believe very strongly in being yourself, but if you're working for someone like this and you depend on her to give you raises and promotions, you're going to have to please her to some extent. Nothing works as well with this type as emulation. Clover will rarely say nice things about you to her superiors, so you'll have to make them notice you on your own, in a way that won't incur her wrath. And you'll want to get out of Clover's reach as soon as possible. It's self-flagellation to work for somebody like Clover for any substantial period of time. You certainly can't complain to the boss, because even if she's understanding, she'll never act on your complaint. She will only think you can't get along with people she likes.

SCENARIO TWO

Emily has just completed the year-end financial report for Thrust Record Stores. She's quite pleased with it and submits it to her boss, Jab Johnson. Jab is thrilled with it. "Emily! You did a fabulous job on this report! I love it. You're the best. Fantastic!" Jab enthuses to Emily, hugging her so hard she loses her balance. *Jab is so terrific,* Emily thinks to herself after he leaves, *I'm really lucky to work for such a positive, sensitive boss.*

Two weeks later, Emily hands in the five-year fiscal plan that's always due after the year-end financials. She's pretty confident that Jab will like it, although there are a few places where she thinks she could have done a little more research. She just didn't have the time. In any case, Jab is a great guy. *No problem,* she thinks, *even if he does have criticisms.*

"*Emily,*" Jab yells as he barrels into her office, "this report is completely unacceptable! What do you think we're running here, a playground? I had to spend two hours marking out changes—two hours I don't have. Fix it this afternoon and have the revised version on my desk by six." Jab storms out, and Emily hears him say "stupid" under his breath. She's stunned, and looks over the bright red, angry marks all over her report. *What happened?* she thinks. *Am I crazy, or was he in love with me just a few days ago?*

Hurricane Harry or Hanna

Hysterical people can be fun to work for, but they can also be weak, unpredictable nightmares with impulse control issues. They're smart, but they don't always use their intelligence to make decisions or judgments. They can also be inattentive and have difficulty focusing on matters at hand. Most of their reactions are based on impressions and feelings, not on the facts. Since they are emotional and don't want to spend too much time thinking about and considering a problem, they will often listen to only one side of a story and make a decision based on incomplete information. They have difficulty in following through, they jump to conclusions, and they idealize situations to such a degree that when things don't work out the way they had imagined, they are severely disappointed and angry. Love and hate come easily to them and are interchangeable, depending on their whim. The problem with working for a hysterical person is that you're never really sure whether you're being judged on your work or the person's feelings about you at that moment. It's always a combination of both, and often, it's only the latter.

Jab Johnson is a **Hurricane Harry**. He's highly intelligent and can be charming, but he can also be quite mean and unsociable. Jab runs a large chain of record stores. There are at least sixty stores all across the country and several in Europe that Jab has to look after and worry about. This is the perfect job for Mr. Johnson because it allows him to shift his attention constantly from one store to another, without ever having to focus on one problem for a long time, which would drive him crazy.

The people who work directly for Jab are a frustrated bunch, because they never know what mood they'll find him in. So, unconsciously, they are always edgy and cranky and angry. Walk through Jab's promotion department on any given day, and you will see office after office of angry, drawn, and scowling faces. Uptight body language is rampant here, and if you ask someone a question, you may only get an icy stare or a sarcastic snort for an answer.

This is one way of dealing with a HH person, but it would be even better to learn to detach, so that the HH's unpredictable outbursts and moods have little sway with you. Whether he's being critical or complimentary, you must learn that neither comment has any real meaning and must never be taken too seriously. Never, ever clutter up an HH person's life with questions, concerns, or opinions. Actually, it's easy to succeed with an HH: Don't bother trying to predict his moods, don't take him too seriously, and don't ask for his help or advice unless absolutely necessary. Oh, and don't expect him to tell you if he likes your green shirt better than your blue one either.

SCENARIO THREE

Tom has just completed a story about strippers for his magazine. It's a really insightful piece, which is sympathetic toward the women involved in this occupation. He's really proud of it. Gabbi Boucher happens to be working on the issue that's running Tom's piece. She reads it and doesn't like Tom's understanding slant. Tom tries to convince her and the others on the editorial team of the story's merits. After the meeting, Tom sits reflecting in his office, feeling good about the meeting. Everyone understood Tom's passion for a piece he worked so hard on. He thinks they'll end up running the article as is. Gabbi parades into his office with a twisted glower on her face.

"Listen, Tom, you didn't have to make a big deal of that story!" Gabbi badgers, stabbing her pointing finger at him, "It's disgusting. Those girls are prostitutes! You dragged everyone down with you into the gutter by having a meeting about it. It upset everyone!" Gabbi stamps out of Tom's office, leaving him feeling guilty and dirty.

Judgmental Judy or Jack

A JJ is never wrong. She is rigid, unforgiving, superior, opinionated, and mistrustful. She likes to stew about things, and she never forgets slights. She's also suspicious. Gabbi Boucher is the perfect example of a judgmental type.

Gabbi is the manager of new product development and editorial advisor for a magazine publisher. She becomes fixated on her own convictions and projects and has a hard time letting them go after she has made a commitment. Her opinions are always stated with an almost religious fervor that other people find hard to stand up to, even when they do disagree. Her automaton bluntness is alienating and intimidating, and often leaves colleagues feeling it's not worth the trouble to argue. If you disagree with Gabbi and you make it known, she will hold it against you for a very, very, very long time. If you do something that Gabbi considers immoral (people like Gabbi often have very fixed moral codes that have little to do with actual ethics and are based more on their own fears and insecurities), she will take great offense and spread the word that you're not a very nice person, that you have emotional problems, or are perhaps stupid and corrupt.

If someone Gabbi doesn't like (which is almost everyone) succeeds at something, her hate for that person will grow in proportion to his or her achievement. She will pack extra venom into the psychological baggage she brings to work each day. This hate (a word she enjoys using often) is what fuels her own working day. She expends a great deal of energy doing things that will demonstrate her superiority over her colleagues. Does the boss care whether she walks around with a scowl on her face or if she shows open disdain for her colleagues? Of course not! She's producing like crazy! He's getting his money's worth—and that's his bottom line.

To deal with JJ types, you must be direct and unemotional in all interactions with them. You must never tell them anything important and certainly nothing personal, because they are outrageous gossips. The best protection against a Gabbi is to keep your distance and your dignity and be very polite.

If a JJ disagrees with you, chalk it up to experience. This shrew will have no real power over you if you don't allow her opinions to affect your mood. Her attitude and presentation skills are definitely a pain in the butt, though.

SCENARIO FOUR

"I want to know your real feelings about working with me, Joan. I really care," Happi explains to her colleague, a half-smile dripping off her face. "It's really important that we get along and understand each other. I consider you a friend."

Joan goes along with Happi, taking the chance that she may be sincere. It's an opportunity to solve a problem in a professional manner. "Well, Happi, I really feel you're overstepping your boundaries by commenting on my work all the time in meetings or privately to other people. I like working with you, but I want to keep my job separate from yours."

"Well, I'm really glad I know that, Joan. I think I should have some say over your job, and now I know what I'm up against. I'm going to fight for control over your work. But we can still be friends. Business is business, right?"

Joan proceeds directly to the ladies' room to throw up.

Pathological monster
There is no better example of the **Pathological Monster** type than Happi Thomas. Happi works for

the same company as Gabbi. A **PM** must be in control at all times, and she is made of Teflon. Nothing
you say to her will ever stick (she's actually not really
paying attention, anyway—she has more important
things to think about—herself) and nothing that
slides off her is real—but it's definitely coated with
a thick, sticky, synthetic substance that can land on
you like the Valdez oil spill landed on those poor fish
and ducks.

The PM is also vain, selfish, even narcissistic. She
has delusions of grandeur and believes herself to be
special, super-talented, and completely unique in her
abilities. She is very often none of these things. She
is an ordinary person with a deeply serious psychological condition. Many kooks get along very well in
offices. Ponder that, if you will. Can you feel the
chill?

The PM is the most difficult to deal with of all
the types because she is oblivious to her own pathology. She believes in her very fiber that her behavior is normal and acceptable; if it bothers other
people, then they are the ones with the serious problem. Her boss often recognizes her failings, but she
is a performer, so he doesn't mind when she treats
people like children or slaves or imbeciles (even
though it is she who lacks a generous intellectual ca-

pacity). The boss feels sorry for her and may even think she is pathetic and wretched, but her problems aren't his concern, as long as he's getting what he wants out of her.

You must remember that *pathological* is the operative word here. The PM isn't using the same frame of reference that you are; she's not playing with the same deck of cards. When you work with or for one, you must remind yourself of this fact several times a day.

I once had a problem with a PM. The head of another department, George, said to me, "Karen, you know how I deal with Devora? I ignore her. If she says something at a meeting, I pretend I didn't hear it and move on. I don't involve myself with any project she works on. I avoid her and try to speak to her as little as possible." It didn't bother Devora that she was being ignored and avoided by George because she wasn't fully cognizant of his behavior toward her. When I told my boss George's solution to dealing with Devora and wondered if he would like me to do the same, he became very upset, and said "No! That's not true!" There's nothing like being reminded of a problem that you have no intention of solving. In any case, my colleague's advice wasn't bad, it was just too late in the game for me to follow it.

Even if you report to a PM, you can avoid her. Do what you're told to do, stay out of her way, and make yourself shine to other, equally powerful colleagues in your company who have the boss's ear. That way, when the PM gives you trouble, other people may come to your defense, since they will dislike the PM as much if not more than you do. The PM, once she is entrenched in a company, will rarely leave. If she's set up in a place where the boss lets her be odious, obnoxious, and creepy, why would she leave? So you'll find dodging her is the only way to get ahead while working with her. If she's not in your department, you'll be fine if you don't include yourself in any project she's involved in. But keep in mind that a PM is a truly sick person who deserves pity. Pity is often a great way to keep you from being driven crazy by someone you can neither understand nor reason with. You'll feel better about yourself, too.

Scenario Five

Andy needs a decision from Joe Schmuck. He's got to know whether Joe wants to ship all the new rate cards to all the advertisers at once or stagger the mailing. "Joe, what do you think? If we send all of them at once, we'll save money on postage. But if we send them separately, we'll be able to measure response to the new prices and modify the rest if we have to."

"Let's go with the cheaper alternative. No, maybe we should stagger them. No, all at once. Send them all at once, Andy."

"Okay, Joe. Whatever you want."

Andy sends them all at once. He doesn't agree with Joe's decision, but it's not worth getting into a conversation with him about it. It'll just mix Joe up and make it harder for him to decide. Andy just wants to keep Joe comfortable and calm. He thinks Joe is basically an okay guy and wouldn't do anything to harm him.

The reaction to the new rates is bad, and all the advertisers are angry. Joe's boss comes down on him for the decision.

"Andy, you made a really bad decision. We should have staggered the mailing. This is really bad. You're going to have to repair your error."

"But, Joe, you told me . . ."

"I told you to stagger the mailing. Now get out, and start doing something about it!"

Joe feels so much better now that he's passed the buck to somebody else.

Missing Vertebra

Joe Schmuck is a living, breathing example of an MV. Insecurity is at the root of most office evils, and not surprisingly, it is the cause of lying, bullying, defensiveness, and/or meanness in the classic MV. MVs also have trouble making decisions, because they're afraid of making the wrong one and getting in trouble with their boss, who they fear will find out how incompetent they truly are and fire them on the spot.

Joe Schmuck is successful because he has become someone his superiors can depend on to be, according to the fancy of whichever person he's reporting to, a punching bag, a yes man, a buffer against the next layer of employees, or a compliant messenger who is perfect for carrying out dirty work like firing and punishment.

What to do about an MV? Don't worry, it's not that difficult. MVs want to avoid one-on-one dealings as much as possible. If you communicate with Joe infrequently, he will actually appreciate you for it. One thing that you must do, however, when meeting with an MV is to keep notes of all the conversations you have with him and follow up with a memo restating these conversations. MVs are notorious for "forgetting" what was said or changing the facts, so this simple procedure will guarantee the MVs honesty in dealing with you. The other benefit is that the MV won't bother trying to lie to you or bully you. They usually respond positively to a strong, confident, decisive colleague.

People, and not their talents, are what make your office special. Just make sure you know what kind of people they are.

Keep Your Office Organized. (Just Don't Throw Out Anything Important.)

*T*his is really crucial. It seems obvious, but you wouldn't believe how many people don't do it. Of course, you know you should keep copies of every performance review you receive and any other memos that refer to your work record. You should be saving every other scrap of paper, too—anything, and I mean *anything* (no matter how trivial or meaningless it may at first appear), that has something to do—even marginally—with your job. These will come in handy at review time, when you're asking for a raise, a promotion, a special assignment, if someone at work tries to do you in, or if your company ever tries to fire you.

When I advise you to make a record of all conversations and meetings, I emphatically don't mean that you should conceal a tape recorder in your garter belt or shoe. Even I consider that paranoid. What you should do is go out and buy a daily calendar—there are a lot of brands, some expensive, some reasonable. It doesn't matter, just get one that has two pages for each day: one for lists and phone calls, the other for notes.

When you attend a meeting where you're bringing up new ideas, make note of the meeting and the ideas on that day and write down the responses of your colleagues, especially your boss's or senior people's thoughts. When you meet with someone one on one, take the same kind of notes. In this case, you should also repeat what they say, when they say it. This is a real bore and it takes practice, but get in the habit right now. It serves several purposes.

First, it helps you remember everything that went on during a day of meetings and interactions with people. You'll be 100 percent more organized.

Second, it's good ammo to have when a person or two insist they said something different from what they actually said. You can refer to your notes if this happens, and since they probably weren't keeping any, your notes will carry more weight than their memory.

Third, when people see you jotting in your notebook during a meeting, they are much more apt to be honest with you, or at least they'll be more careful about what they say. Some people, however, will never learn and will still say a lot of stupid things. If you write these things down, they can only work to your benefit.

Fourth, keeping notes gives you the proof and therefore the courage to stand up for yourself.

For example, Sally works at a magazine. It's Wednesday, and she's just pitched her boss a terrific story. "That's a wonderful idea, Sally! I think it could work for the May issue. It's just what the editorial board is looking for. I'll get back to you right after Thursday's meeting."

Sally responds, makes a note of what she says in her book, and replies, "I'm so glad you like my idea, Irene. I'm also thrilled you'll get back to me tomorrow afternoon."

Okay, so Sally has reinforced what her boss said and has written it down; now all she has to do is wait. Thursday afternoon rolls around, and Irene's nowhere in sight. Sally waits an extra hour, then goes to Irene's office—perfectly acceptable—after all, she promised! Irene is in her office fidgeting nervously. "Irene, what did the board say?" Irene hems and haws for a few seconds, then blurts out, "They didn't like it Sally, they feel the subject has been done to death. But I want to encourage you in that story direction."

Sally reiterates, "Irene, you're encouraging me in that direction?" It's important to use the same terminology in this situation. "Yes," answers Irene. Sally writes Irene's suggestion down, right then and there. She does this religiously all year to see if a pattern forms. Because it might. I'm going to give this little story two endings that both demonstrate how useful keeping records can be.

ENDING #1

Sally has decided after eight months that she's tired of Irene telling her that her ideas are great, then coming back to say that the board doesn't like them, and then, when Sally asks to be managed or guided, Irene encourages her in the wrong direction. Sally thinks she might be better off reporting to someone else. She makes a discreet appointment to see Bob, Irene's supervisor, and discusses with him professionally and in a low-key manner that she feels she's not getting the direction she needs. When Bob asks why she thinks this, Sally has ready a list of her ideas with the dates she brought them up, the reasons Irene gave her that they were rejected, and notations on Irene's encouragement. Sally does this in a modulated and friendly voice (Truth #2) and presents only facts, not feelings or opinions.

Bob looks the list over, and not surprisingly, there are a couple of ideas that he doesn't recall hearing about that he likes. Most of the other ideas don't sound the way Bob remembers them. Of course, Bob will say nothing disparaging about Irene. He won't even discuss it with her. In fact, Irene will get a good raise this year. But Bob gives Sally some kindly words of advice, assigns her a story to edit, and has her report to Margaret.

Sally is fuming. Irene is such a wimp, a liar, and a coward! But she feels some satisfaction that her diligent note keeping got her what she wanted. However, she makes the mistake of trying to figure out what's wrong with Irene and why she is such a successful slob. Trying to figure out people like Irene can make you a quick candidate for an asylum—and I'm not talking about those fancy ones in Switzerland. Was Irene the last to be picked for the ball team in junior high? Probably. Did everyone make fun of her stomach in high school? Most likely. Has Irene always been unable to make up her mind and give an employee clear direction? A resounding *yes*. Forget about it! It doesn't matter!

So Sally puts Irene out of her mind completely: she no longer exists in Sally's life, and believe me, people like Irene are thrilled to get rid of Sally, who require her to respond to another human being with respect and professionalism, and she isn't capable of this kind of interaction.

ENDING #2:

At review time, Sally is scolded and warned by Irene (who, like most cowards, is also a bully), that she's not coming up with enough good ideas. Irene puts Sally on three-month warning and hands her her review to sign. Sally takes the review back to her office and doesn't sign it. Instead, she brings it back to the office, writes a memo, and copies to Bob. Do I have to tell you what the memo says? She attaches her idea list with her dispute of the review and delivers it to Irene and Bob. Sally is taken off warning and reassigned to Margaret and gets a good raise. Irene, of course, also receives a good raise that year and a comforting pat on the head from Bob. Bob feels sorry for Irene, and at any rate, she doesn't make waves.

Sally keeps all the paperwork from this fiasco in a special file at home. What if Sally hadn't kept notes? It would have been Sally's manager's word against hers, and management's word would have won out.

You don't have to work for a magazine for something like this to happen to you. This truth is important, whether you work at a salt pork factory or an accounting firm. Similar scenarios happen all the time, everywhere. Dunderheads like Irene are what I call an **Office Disease (OD)**—and all offices have caught it. It's an epidemic.

It's obvious by now why taking note of oral exchanges about your performance, your work habits, your ideas, or your shortcomings is important. Don't be lazy. Start taking notes now!

My friend Henry works in new product development for a cosmetic company. He once got a note from his boss after having lunch with her and an outside client. The note said, "You're sensational and a tremendous asset to the company!" That note proved extremely valuable and important to him eight months later.

Henry also received a holiday card from someone he had done some work with. This person had enclosed with it a glass angel tree ornament. The note said, "You're an angel, you made this project a

dream." My friend saved both the note and the angel. And guess what? Like the letter from his boss, it
came in very handy—along with all the other similar
notes he had received at his job.

Henry's company wanted to fire him for arbitrary
reasons involving the projects he was working on.
The company didn't feel the projects were profitable,
and they blamed Henry. The projects, however, were
handed over to Henry from his boss. He was not
assigned to do original work (although he was capable of it). His boss illustrated the financial shortcomings of Henry's projects to management as a way
to get rid of him. However, Henry was able to defend
himself. The notes he saved and the commendations
from many people both inside and outside of the
company came to his defense. He also saved the notes
and memos that accompanied the work his boss
passed on to him. These informal notes from Henry's
boss and the compliments from others were even
more important than his reviews, because they had
been voluntary and offered freely; they were passed
on to him with sincerity. The documents also proved
that Henry's manager handled the situation badly
and unprofessionally. If Henry hadn't kept those various notes—everything from official memos to notes
scribbled on used yellow Post-its—things would not

have turned out as well for him. Henry kept his job and is now working on original—and successful—projects.

Notes of thanks and praise from your colleagues or outside people are called **commendations**. Most police departments in the country file letters written by citizens, bad or good, about police officers, and put them in their individual files. These count a lot when the police officer comes up for review. Do this for yourself. If your superior passes on a letter of praise about you from someone else, keep it. Even if you get a holiday card from someone you worked with and they mention how great you are, save that, too. It all counts. Any small sentence of praise scribbled on a Post-it left on your desk or written on a memo you wrote that was sent back to you is important. Don't feel silly. Often, things said indirectly or that are scribbled in the margin of a note or memo can end up being more meaningful, important, and powerful than official memos. You should also save copies of all memos and notes that you write. Keep all these documents filed and categorized. Keep your documents filed and categorized in a system that you find easy to use. One simple way is organizing memos and paperwork by the individual it concerns or was received from. Subcategories within that file should be ordered by 1) date received and 2) subject (job performance, personal comments, meeting notes, etc.). But I know you're busy, so just keeping the stuff in some kind of recognizable order is good enough if you can't handle that kind of detailed filing.

If something does happen, and you don't have any documents that show your side of the story, you're out of luck. Keeping a file is like having an insurance policy. You hope you'll never have to use it, but you'll be glad you have it if you do.

Documentation is also essential when one of your colleagues or superiors lies, and you somehow get mixed up in it. If it's a work lie and you have documentation to prove them wrong (or notes from a conversation), use them. They won't screw around with you again. The same thing goes if someone tries to pass the buck of blame on to you. And, of course, a good file of evidence is invaluable when you're fired (see Truth #12).

You should never turn the other cheek or look the other way when someone falsely represents you or passes you over for a special assignment or deserved promotion. I believe in direct face-to-face encounters when this happens, and having documentation only gives your argument more weight. Even if you don't get the results you want the first time, the next time you will be taken more seriously.

A good file of commendations and records of your performance is useful when requesting a raise or promotion. It is always impressive to have tangible proof that you've done a good job (most managers will forget), how you were praised for it, and who did the praising.

Before your review comes up, type a memo explaining what you've accomplished, including the praise of your clients, colleagues, and superiors. Keep it short, concise, and focused. This works like magic, especially since you can't expect your employer to remember every wonderful thing you've done in the past year.

Keeping your paperwork in order is time consuming, but it's really very simple. Make an appointment with yourself today to organize your file.

Forget what organization experts tell you. Read it once, and if it has anything to do with you, *keep it in a file at home*. You will be very happy that you did.

Gossip as Much as You Want. (But Don't Tell Anyone Anything.)

Who was it who said history was just a bunch of gossip? I can't remember, but whoever it was, was right. Everyone gossips, day in and day out. It's hard to resist telling a juicy secret to a friend or office mate, especially when it involves someone you don't like. I'm realistic; I'm not going to tell you not to do it. But you must do it carefully and with thought. Therein lies the power of gossip. Otherwise, gossip can become a dangerous and intoxicating drug.

There are always a few people in the know at work. They seem to know who's getting hired and fired before the memo is distributed. They know who's pregnant and who's getting a divorce. They know who hates whom, and how everyone ranks. How do they gather all this information? By cultivating the people who have the information they want. Can you be successful by staying out of the gossip fray? Yes, but gossip is a big part of office life, and some of it can actually be helpful.

Gossip should be used to protect and to promote yourself, not to destroy others. However, there will be those in your office who will use it cruelly, so you must learn to be aware of these people.

Gabbi Boucher is a fine example of an intelligent, clever, and cruel gossip collector. Gabbi has made her way to the top not only by making some smart decisions but by using the knowledge gossip has given her. She also uses gossip to undermine colleagues she dislikes.

The first thing Gabbi Boucher does when a new person arrives in her department is take the newcomer out to lunch. She wants to get to know the person. In other words, she has a repertoire of questions she asks to find out as much as she possibly can about the newcomer professionally and personally. Gabbi has a well-honed enthusiastic and concerned tone of voice (Truth #2) that she uses with her victims, in this case Shelley. Here is an annotated list of questions Gabbi asks Shelley to draw her out:

Describe what you did before you came here. It sounds so interesting.

Gabbi really is interested in Shelley's answer. This information is important. Gabbi learns about Shelley's job and her experience, thereby inferring how much of a professional threat she will be to Gabbi.

Did you like your colleagues at your old job?

Although Shelley is not going to be completely honest right away, Gabbi can tell how much information she will eventually be able to get out of Shelley by the answer she gives. Any hints Shelley gives about her real feelings are indications that Gabbi will be able to get more out of Shelley later. If Shelley is very closemouthed, Gabbi knows she'll have a tougher time, and it's up to her to decide whether Shelley is worth pursuing.

How do you like the office so far?

Again, Gabbi will infer things. Here's an opportunity to see if Shelley feels the same way about certain people as she does. Most importantly, this is the time for Gabbi to start planting the seeds of her opinions about other people in the office in Shelley's mind.

Where do you live?

The answer to this simple, innocuous question gives Gabbi an entrée into finding out if Shelley is married, has a partner, is in a relationship, has children, is well off or middle class. Once you start talking about where you live, it makes it a lot easier to start talking about other basic personal facts.

What are your goals? What do you hope to accomplish?

Her answer will give Gabbi an indication of how ambitious Shelley is. Again, Gabbi can estimate whether Shelley will be an ally or a competitor.

Gabbi's real skill isn't in asking the questions, since they're pretty basic and not very imaginative, but rather in her ability to listen and intuit, to read between the lines. She can get a pretty good profile of her new prey over a pleasant hour-and-a-half lunch.

Next, everyone comes to Gabbi to find out about the new girl. This is an important step in Gabbi's strategy. She becomes the center of all **unofficial information. Unofficial information** is anything not announced from the company pulpit (and is not specifically necessary to do your job), that can help you categorize and deal with the person you are scoping out. Gabbi's power base increases because she's recognized as someone who just knows everything. Having a strong power base among employees is very important. Gabbi is also known as a gossip, so smart people are careful about what they tell her. On the other hand, if they want a piece of information broadcast around the office in eighteen hours or less, they tell Gabbi.

Jack, a colleague of Gabbi's, was going to resign and take another job. During his lunch break, he imprudently told her this, asking her not to tell anyone until he'd had a chance to spread the news himself. Did she keep the promise? What do you think? By the end of the day, everyone in the office knew Jack was leaving. Gabbi stole his chance to tell his friends and coworkers himself. He should have known better.

Gabbi does keep some information close to the cuff: facts about herself (gossips rarely divulge anything about themselves) and about her superiors. She uses this private data to help her with particular goals: to get something she wants, to stonewall some event she doesn't like, or to cripple another person's chances of getting ahead. This is called **selective gossiping.** It's knowing what to say and what to leave out in order to control the reactions of your coworkers.

Another way Gabbi collects gossip is to cultivate

as many assistants as she can. Some assistants are outstanding and will not give out information about their bosses. This is the kind of assistant you want (Truth #5). Gabbi's nice to those assistants, but she spends more time with the really gossipy ones— they're usually unhappy in their jobs or dislike their bosses. It's easy to tell which ones these are by their attitudes. Most assistants have not developed the professional skill of covering up their disdain for someone they dislike. Gabbi's technique is to show interest in their lives or careers and she will counsel them often.

Gabbi establishes herself as a concerned person who wants to help. She feeds the assistants harmless gossip that they perceive as being juicy, thus establishing trust and bonding. The other thing she does is take them out to an occasional lunch or has it sent up to her office for a "picnic."

What does she learn from the assistants? Everything from embarrassing personal habits to what's in their bosses' confidential envelopes. There's one secretary in Gabbi's office who tells her every single time she has to buy laxatives for her boss. She hates this task, so this is her way of getting back at the boss. This information may seem trivial, but it tells Gabbi the boss is probably very uptight and can't relax. She uses this to build a better profile of him, thereby enabling her to read him and play him effectively.

Gabbi also likes to learn who is considered a star and who's getting the shaft by the executives. She learns from her boss's assistant that the president of the company wants to get rid of one of her colleagues. This is a person Gabbi happens to like, so in an act of kindness, Gabbi doesn't tell her she's about to be fired, but she does give her some very helpful and specific hints about what she can do to defend herself and her standing in the office. This actually works, so gossip saves the day. She keeps her job.

Of course, if Gabbi hadn't liked this person, she would have spread the word to a few people, who of course would start to avoid this person like the plague—no one likes hanging around a loser. So, the boss not only loses confidence in this person's work, he sees that her colleagues aren't interested in her, either, thereby eliminating any guilt he would have over this decision ("No one likes her anyway"—another reason to fire her, she's not compatible with her coworkers). She gets the ax the following week.

Gabbi has achieved an excellent balance of collecting and spreading gossip. Mostly, she uses gossip for her own gain. Gabbi is competing with Joe for a promotion. Gabbi can't stand Joe. In fact, she has used the word *hate* when describing her feelings about him to her allies at work. She thinks Joe is incompetent and foolish. Gabbi sets out to uncover as much dirt about Joe as she can. She gets to know people who had worked with Joe in other situations and offices. She finds out he had the same decision-making problems and logical reasoning issues as he does at his present job. These are known weaknesses within their industry. Joe has a history of being wishy-washy and indecisive. In response, Gabbi finds ways to force Joe to make decisions in front of the boss, which of course he can't do. By doing this, Gabbi illustrates Joe's inability to the boss, at the same time demonstrating her own strong decision-making abilities.

Alone with the boss, she lets it slip out in a casual and caring way that Joe has always had this problem, letting him know that the chances of Joe changing or growing are pretty slim. The boss sees Gabbi as a much better decision maker. Gabbi gets the coveted job. Even if the boss is aware of Gabbi's game—and he is—he doesn't care. He enjoys seeing his employees squabble and compete, as long as it doesn't interfere with his day. After all, it *is* survival of the fittest, isn't it?

Another example of Gabbi's ability to undermine people is how she treats a fellow executive, Sarah. Gabbi doesn't like Sarah. She thinks Sarah is mean, selfish, ungrateful, and unpleasant (takes one to know one). She finds out as much about Sarah from Sarah's assistant as she can. She encourages her own assistant to make friends with the other assistants, so that her assistant can report back to her with even more information. She spreads some ugly stories about Sarah. Sarah won't get fired, but she won't be well-liked by others. A lot of people say that work isn't a popularity contest, but in a way, it is. If people don't like you, they aren't going to tell you anything or go out of their way to help you. It's just a different kind of popularity than in social life.

Knowing naughty things about Sarah makes Gabbi feel better about herself, and it helps Gabbi establish an effective way of dealing with Sarah. Knowing Sarah's frailties and weaknesses removes any threat that Gabbi may feel from her. Sarah's only human and this information allows Gabbi to push Sarah's buttons. Knowing the things that make Sarah uncomfortable or irritable will come in handy during important meetings or confrontations.

Gossip is different in different kinds of businesses. I think any communications industry runs more on gossip, than say, accounting firms. But wherever you work, it's important to know how to get gossip and how to withhold it. Personal information should be kept private as it can be used against you more easily than professional gossip. For example, Gabbi knows that Fred likes to drink a lot. She knows this from observing him at Christmas parties and other company functions where liquor is served. She notices that he can really put it away. Fred is not an obvious drunk nor does he engage in embarrassing behavior when loaded. However, Gabbi knows that the upper management does not like executives to engage in behavior that could be unprofessional or embarrassing. Gabbi wants Fred out of her way as he is interfering in a project that she wants control over at work. Since she knows she can't get this control in the conventional way, by asking for it, she has to attack Fred were it counts.

She starts spreading the rumor that Fred is a secret alcoholic. She doesn't tell her superiors this, but she does tell their assistants and other carefully chosen underlings she knows she can count on to spread hearsay like wildfire. Though Fred has never exhibited any bad behavior while drinking, his boss and the upper management team eventually hear of this rumor and take Fred off the project, ostracizing him until he eventually finds another job and quits. Gabbi has won again. Fred needs to learn never to drink anywhere near his coworkers.

Gabbi is Machiavellian in the extreme. She isn't in the habit of ruining people's careers just for the fun of it. She is selective about her targets. But she does keep people's bad habits and personal failings in her head in case such a desire arises. Frankly, I think it's a waste of time to be this involved in the details of your colleagues lives and work, but you must be aware of people like Gabbi and how they operate. Never try to be a friend to the likes of Gabbi.

There is a good side to gossip—the kind of professional gossip that lets you know about job openings, what the competition is doing, or how your business is performing. All this information is useful and can have a direct impact on your job. That's the only kind of gossip you should keep your ears open to and act on. Because Gabbi's methods, unless you are smart enough to make them work and you can live with yourself, will ultimately fail you. Believe me, the Gabbis of the world are very sad and angry people.

THE DANGER OF GOSSIP

Gossip is like undetected cancer—you don't know the damage it's done until it's too late. Gossip can be harmful even when you're not the one being gossiped about.

Case in point: Shelley is having trouble with Happi Thomas. Shelley is beside herself because she's never encountered someone quite like Happi before, and she needs advice. So she goes to Gabbi, who has always shown concern for Shelley ever since they had lunch on her first day of work, for help. Gabbi, of course, hates Happi Thomas and will take any opportunity to rag on her. So when Shelley comes to Gabbi, she is thrilled to tell her every awful, gory, personal and professional detail she knows about Happi. Her parting advice? "Don't let Happi get to you."

Shelley leaves the office depressed because, based on Gabbi's descriptions, she's wondering how someone as screwed up as Happi can have such an influential job. It's also hard not to let someone get to you when you know the freakish details of that person's life. Stay away from this kind of gossip. It can only make you crazy and miserable.

Meanwhile, Gabbi wastes no time telling her colleagues that Shelley has a problem with Happi. Happi is not well liked, and so her coworkers are glad to know there is yet another person on their team. They hope there's a fight, because it's so much fun to watch. To help the process along, they feed Shelley even more unflattering information about Happi. Now Shelley is being inundated with Horrors of Happi, and it is not helping her one bit. But Shelley listens, nonetheless. It's sort of like driving by an accident; you don't want to look, but you can't resist. If she'd been smart, Shelley would never have solicited anyone's advice, especially Gabbi's.

Gabbi knows that the boss is fond of Shelley, so she hopes that all this negative information will filter its way through Shelley to the boss. That way, Gabbi doesn't have to do it herself. You see, Gabbi is the kind of person who doesn't really want to set you on fire, but she won't throw water on you if you're burning.

In the end, it all backfires. Happi doesn't care if

no one likes her, so it doesn't matter to her what people are saying, and the boss really doesn't care one way or another as long as Happi gets her job done and doesn't bring him many complaints.

Shelley feels alone and confused, and she is unable to shut off the stream of Happi Madness that has found its way to her door. She's now an emotional wreck because Happi is getting to her and there's nowhere for her to turn. This has damaged her professionally, but all her colleagues have enjoyed the intrigue, drama, and confusion they created. In the end, they abandon Shelley because she's depressed all the time. Who needs that?

The moral? Stay away from Gabbi-style gossip. As soon as you hear it, leave the room. It's really more about the gossiper than the gossipee, anyway. And rest assured, Gabbi'll be doing the same thing to you someday.

Remember that no one, not even your closest colleagues, will keep a confidence—even if they promise to. Guaranteed, they'll tell at least one other person and it'll go from there. Of course, you can take my mother's advice, and not give people anything to talk about. You know, be discreet.

If people are talking about you, it means one of

two things: Either you're a very interesting individual (I'm sure you are!), or the people doing the talking have no life. Finally, there really is no such thing as bad publicity.

Gossip can serve as both a protection and as a weapon. Proceed with caution.

Be Good to Your Assistant (or the Whole Office Will Know You're a Wreck).

$\mathcal{S}$o much of your day is spent with your assistant—more time, perhaps, than you spend with your family—that it's imperative you feel comfortable with this person. But you shouldn't be friends with your assistant. More women than men fall into this trap. Being friends blurs the lines of work and duty and makes the senior/junior worker dynamic unnecessarily complex.

THE THREE THINGS YOU WANT FROM AN ASSISTANT

1. He/she should perform all necessary work duties defined by you.

2. He/she must be completely discreet about mail, phone calls, screaming fits, hangovers, and embarrassing and visible stains on your clothes.

3. He/she must be completely forthcoming with all information gathered from other assistants, stray memos, etc., that pertains to your business.

Hire the right person, and your life will change dramatically.

SIGNS YOU MAY WANT TO HIRE SOMEONE

A graduate from a state or local university rather than a fancy school

Why not hire someone with a glamorous background? Well, I'm going to get in trouble for saying this, but it's been my experience and the experience of many people I know that having a privileged college graduate working for you is sometimes more trouble than it's worth. Often, these people feel that since they have a diploma from a prestigious university and have interned in their father's accounting firm or TV production company, they need to be promoted within six months, or feel certain kinds of work (like all the work contained in their job description) are beneath them. I realize this is a generalization, but I've heard this scenario so many times that it is worthy of mention.

Many people will be impressed by a fancy school on a résumé, and they have that right. But remember, people don't go to fancy schools to get an education. If all they wanted was an education, reading a lot of books or attending a state university would suffice. They go to make the all-important connections. You want someone smart, not someone who's on a first-name basis with Henry Kissinger.

Another scenario: Your superior has gone to the same school as your assistant, or wishes he or she had gone to that school, or maybe his kids go to that school, so he ends up taking a special liking to your assistant. This could be inconvenient for you.

My friend Diana has a good example of this. She works for the print media department of a large public relations firm. She hired a sweet young woman, Alice, right out of an Ivy League school that the department head admired because of the university's sports team. When Alice discovered this, she became a fan of her college team overnight (even though while she was attending school she couldn't have cared less). In turn, the boss became enamored of her:

she was so sweet, cute, loved sports, and she was twenty-two. Perfect, right? No. She was a lousy worker. She couldn't follow directions or get anything done on time, if ever. Because the boss had such a crush on Alice, Diana couldn't fire her. Once Alice even said, "Oh, I have Lenny wrapped around my finger!" Diana, at her wits' end, ended up giving Alice a promotion and lessening her workload. Now, does Alice know the twelve truths, or what? My prediction is that in another year, she'll have another promotion, have even less work to do, and be making more money. If she sticks around long enough, she may eventually run the company. You definitely do not want an assistant like Alice.

A good assistant must have humility but not lack confidence, be smart but not a smart-ass, and be diligent with any work you assign but not be simpering about it. I have found that graduates of state colleges and universities have more of these qualities than Ivy League or private university graduates.

Job Experience Includes a Wide Variety of Employment

Why is having job experience not related to the job at hand important? Because it shows diversity. Some fancy school people I've met don't have a clue about actually working and dealing with the public. I think someone who's been a short-order cook or sold pretzels from a cart or handled animals at a petting zoo—or any other job that young people get when Daddy can't get them an internship at MGM— makes them develop a sense of understanding and tolerance.

I once worked in an admissions office of one of the top law schools in the country. My job was to go through incoming admissions, file them according to certain benign categories, and to make appointments for candidates to meet with the admissions dean. One day I told the dean how amazing I thought some of these students were: straight A's, internships at law firms, Ivy League B.A.'s, perfect test scores, yearly trips to Europe. Do you know what he said? "Karen, those are the ones you have to watch out for. They're too perfect and often have problems coping. They won't make the best law students or the greatest lawyers." He went on to explain that the students who wrote powerful essays, but maybe had a couple of C's, average test scores, and had useful job experience, such as working in a health clinic in the inner city, waiting on customers in an ice cream shop, cleaning stables at the race track, had a much better chance at being distinguished lawyers. The "perfect" person's expectations and views on life are often unrealistic in ways that won't be helpful to others. Moral: You want to hire a real person.

Inconspicuous Appearance

You don't want your assistant to stick out like a sore thumb. By blending in, your assistant can more easily gather the information you need. Your assistant will probably have an easier time of it, too. So, unless you're hiring an assistant for a tattoo parlor, let the guy with the nose ring look elsewhere.

Must Speak Clearly

Good diction is very important because your assistant is going to be doing a lot of talking for you. If you can't understand what this person is saying during an interview, what makes you think anyone else will?

INTERVIEW TIP-OFFS THAT MAY INDICATE A CANDIDATE'S WEAKNESS

1. Arms crossed over the chest for the entire meeting

2. Clenching and unclenching fists while you both talk

3. Chewing on anything: pen, pencils, gum, erasers, nails, or hair

4. Fidgeting in the seat

5. Covering his or her mouth when speaking

6. Avoiding eye contact

Once they're working for you, never belittle, nag, or insult them, and don't make them cry. Make their duties very clear. Be honest about what you expect of them. Include everything so they won't give you dirty looks after spending half the day at the photocopy machine. If they do something wrong, tell them directly and immediately and move on. Don't harp. Praise them when their work is good (this goes a long way in establishing loyalty). Promote them and give them raises when earned. Champion them. They will tell you everything. But if someone doesn't respond to your good treatment, get rid of him ASAP. Who needs an ingrate?

Always respond to your assistant if she asks you a question, presents you with an idea, or needs advice in handling a work issue. If you don't, or if you expect her to work it out herself, you are asking for trouble. An assistant who feels invisible will become unhappy very quickly and will turn on you. If you are a boss who treats your assistant like an indentured servant, you may think you have loyalty, but take it from me, you have no idea what's slipping out of your office when your back is turned. Disloyalty is even worse than mediocre work. In no time at all, everyone will know that you're fighting with your spouse, your beach house is sinking, you're drinking too much, or that you're getting chewed out by your boss.

Chemistry is one of those obnoxious words that's used to describe all kinds of good and bad relationships. "The chemistry's just not right between us, Joan, so I'm ditching you for another woman." "The chemistry between you and this company is just not clicking, Ed, so we're going to have to let you go." It's a vague term that simply means someone either likes you or doesn't. But good chemistry is always important to have with your assistant. It may take a couple of months to develop, but start cultivating it right away.

Have you ever seen the movie called *All about Eve*? If not, rent it. Eve Harrington, the title character, is the ultimate Assistant from Hell. If you suspect that your assistant is turning into an **Eve** or **Evan Harrington,** you'll want to start ridding this odious person from your life pronto. Here are some clues that you may have an **EH** working for you:

1. She doesn't tell you any valuable information, and when you tell her some office news, she says, "I know, I heard that yesterday."

2. An EH sends memos to your boss or other higher ups without your knowledge, consent, or approval.

3. She has lunch alone with your boss.

4. She starts dressing better than you do.

5. She takes more than an hour for lunch when she doesn't have a doctor's appointment.

6. She is always chatting with your colleagues but stops as soon as you walk in the room.

Don't let an E.H. open your mail, don't conduct business or personal conversations in front of one, and under no circumstances confide about issues at work. An E.H. won't necessarily do you any harm in the long run, but it's a pain in the ass to have one around, so why bother?

Good assistants are worth their weight in gold. Do not neglect good workers, and reward them for their loyalty.

Take Orders—But Only from Your Boss.

I know this seems obvious, but think about it. Most people you know, yourself included, end up doing someone else's work at some point in their career and kick themselves later for being so stupid. It's easy to fall into this trap because either you don't realize at the time that you're doing somebody else's job, or you think it will help you get extra points, praise, promotions, or raises. Wrong.

The only extra work you should ever do is that which will have a direct, positive effect on your future. For example, it's much wiser to perfect your résumé in your spare moments than it is to write pitch letters for the sales manager when you report to the marketing manager. Get it?

Give someone an inch, and they'll take a mile. If the sales manager has you writing letters, next thing you'll be helping her with financial reports, and then the year-end statement and so on and so on until you're exhausted and hating yourself because nothing is happening in your career—but she is taking a Caribbean cruise to celebrate her recent promotion.

Psychologically, people will think of you as a doormat. Even if it's unconscious, it's floating around in the back of their minds. When you're not focused entirely on your job, you can't move yourself forward. So no matter what the sales manager says about it being helpful to your career (it's in her best interests to tell you this), it ain't. Most successful people I know do only what's required of them.

Sheila is such a woman. She runs the very large sales department of a computer company. Over the years, she has built up her department and has added many subdepartments to her realm. This has been an excellent way for her to become powerful. The more people reporting to you, the better.

The interesting thing about Sheila and the people in her department is that they never seem to do anything. They must generate sales, but I don't have a clue how. Sheila's desk is always spotless. There's not a scrap of paper in sight, not even a phone message. There are no personal effects of any kind. In fact, her office looks like one of those temporary executive offices they put roving ex-VPs in—and she's rarely in it. She's usually at the gym, running errands, on a "business trip," or at home with her baby. The only woman I used to see in this department on a regular basis was usually on the telephone with her friends, filing her nails, or playing with her huge and elaborate earrings. She also never had any paper on her desk.

Whenever I saw Sheila in the elevator and we got to talking about work, she would always brag, "Bob (the president) always says to me, 'I never worry about you, Sheila, you run the best department.' He always cancels our weekly meetings because he knows everything is going great." Why? Because Sheila does only what is required and expects that same basic work from her employees. Not bothering herself with other people's assignments cuts down on her anxiety level, too. The fewer people you're doing things for, the fewer people you have to worry about pleasing. Sheila pleases only one person: herself. Everybody else can go to hell.

Sheila's department generates enough income that Bob is happy. She doesn't care when or how her people do the work, she just tells them what she wants, and she's only interested in the results. Since her employees have free reign as long as they get their jobs done, they're happy. When Sheila does have a meeting with Bob, she shows him sales figures, tells him what the department is working on, and says, "Everything is terrific Bob, no problem." She can answer any questions Bob has, because she knows more about her job than he does. Bob has a tremendous feeling of peace and security after talking to Sheila because everyone else who reports to him has a litany of complaints and problems.

Sheila may not be making as much money for the company as she could, but why should she? Because she does the minimum that makes the boss happy, always seems positive about her department, and her people seem happy enough, the boss thinks she is doing a marvelous job. In his mind, all those things are more important than bigger profits. Anything that makes his life easier is worth a lot.

Eighty-five percent of Sheila's success is based on keeping her boss appeased, rather than on working like a maniac to make loads of sales in order to impress him. We can all learn from Sheila, who makes a huge salary and owns six (no kidding) fur coats. They may be vulgar, but you get the point.

"Work hard and you'll succeed" is one of the biggest lies ever perpetrated, usually by people I call **Bloodsuckers. Bloodsuckers** are everywhere, and you will always be running into them. Learn to identify them, and steer clear of them before they reach your throat. **Bloodsuckers** don't look like monsters or vampires (although some can). You might even think that they're nice, they seem so harmless. They're not. Under that seemingly sweet, innocent exterior is a selfish person with only personal interests at heart who will use you in any way possible to make his or her life more convenient and comfortable.

One way of identifying a **Bloodsucker** is by gossip (Truth # 6). Find out what others think of her if you suspect she might be one. Also, a **BS** can be immediately identified if she couches left-handed compliments or says bitchy, nasty things in a nice context. As in, "Well, if I had legs like yours, I'd wear inappropriately short skirts, too," or "Gosh, I thought you were forty, you're so mature—not that you *look* forty!"

Bloodsuckers are miserable and insecure, and these are the qualities that propel them forward. This is what they do in order to get even with the bad hand they think has been dealt them. They will never see anything wrong with any of their behavior, and will seem genuinely bewildered and puzzled if you point it out to them.

Never allow a **Bloodsucker** to get close to you or

befriend you. A classic example of a **Bloodsucker** is Lucretia, a woman who runs the art department of a major magazine. Lucretia is very ambitious, and always feels like whatever she has is not enough. She has a fancy VP title, and feels this entitles her to expect those around her to give her deferential treatment. Hard to believe, since there are about fifteen other VPs in her company. In this particular case, the VP title is a bone that's thrown to discontented senior management.

Lucretia's frustration has stoked in her a burning desire to get into the editorial department of her magazine. She feels the art people are not respected, and this fuels her insecurity. She believes her status would be improved if she could add an editorial feather to her cap. She also thinks she's just as smart as those snobs in the editorial department. Lucretia knows the only way for her to get ahead is to learn something about the editorial area, which does not include—*and this is important*—doing anything for them. She wants to be in the position of telling the editorial people what to do. This is the best route to more power, and so she must come up with a way to accomplish it.

The magazine wants to put out two special holiday issues a year, along with their usual twelve issues. This is the opportunity that Lucretia has been waiting for. Lucretia explains to her boss that she would be a good person to oversee these issues, because they will be artistic, in keeping with the holiday spirit. The boss says okay quickly because he wants to get the work off his back. Anyway, Lucretia has always been loyal to him, and she always seems to bounce back after any arguments they may have.

The only problem is, Lucretia isn't very good at writing, and this job requires a lot of it. The boss knows this, but doesn't think about it. His favorite saying is, "Make it work," which he firmly asserts is an inspiring and helpful philosophy of almost mystical potency. In other words: "I don't care how you get it done, just do it and don't bug me about it." Since all the people who report to Lucretia are in the art department, they can't write that well, either (not to disparage artists, it's just a fact in this particular case). So, she needs to find someone in the editorial department to do the work for her.

She immediately thinks of Elaine and her assistant Jim. Elaine is smart, fast, and efficient. Jim is talented, young, and eager. Lucretia asks her boss if Elaine can help out with the special issues. The boss says yes, if Elaine wants to do it, but it's not required. So, Lucretia drops by Elaine's office and gives her the good news: Lucretia has chosen Elaine to help out with the special issues because Elaine and Jim are so terrific and Lucretia feels a special bond with Elaine. Plus, the boss thinks it's a great idea! Elaine stupidly feels flattered, thinking that working on the special issue might be good for her career.

Elaine and Jim start to work with Lucretia. Lucretia asks Jim if he can write the captions and copy (Lucretia's responsibility). She wants Elaine to write the editorial/marketing profile of the project for the sales department and create, assign, and edit all the freelance material (also Lucretia's responsibility). Jim and Elaine spend extra hours on this and come up with fine results. Lucretia tells them how this extra work will do wonders for their careers. Elaine and Jim eventually find themselves under the jurisdiction of Lucretia, whom neither of them officially report to.

When Elaine and Jim decide that they've had enough, which is pretty late in the game, they go to Lucretia and insist that she learn how to write the material herself. After all, if she wants to be in editorial, she should know what she's doing. Okay, here's the good part. Lucretia incredulously replies, "Elaine, I'm a vice president, and even though I may not be an expert in your job, you should defer to me as your superior. I am a special kind of editorial person and should not be expected to do this work. It is my job to direct you." Wait! There's more! Lucretia also accuses Elaine of being selfish and not having the best interests of the company at heart, "which is, after all, what you're paid for." On top of that, Lucretia says she is hurt by Elaine's comments. Bringing up feelings is a favorite guilt inducer used by BSs. Is the blood drained yet?

At last, Elaine and Jim get the full picture; the lightbulb flashes on over their heads. Too bad it's too late. Lucretia gets the credit for the fabulous editorial job on the special issues, with her name at the top of the masthead as both editorial director and creative director. After all, she was heading up the project and directed the editorial. She got to look things over and say yes or no, which added an extra ten minutes to her day. Plus, Elaine and Jim were seen by the boss as drones who were able to carry out Lucretia's remarkable ideas and insights to perfection—a great reflection on Lucretia's ability to convey ideas and manage people. Not only that, but shrewdly, Lucretia was able to get two people from another important department to report to her without their knowledge. Lucretia did not really do any extra work, she just got credit for it—and that had a direct and positive effect on her job.

Elaine and Jim were duped, but it's their own fault. They should have said no to Lucretia, as everyone else in the editorial department would have because they had already had similar experiences with the company BS. They didn't listen to their colleagues' warnings. They entered into the arrangement because Lucretia seemed sincere and committed to helping them with their careers. They received no extra credit, no promotions, no rewards, and no praise for their efforts. After all, they weren't doing it for their real boss. He didn't care as long as they were getting his work done. In fact, they might have gotten into trouble with him if they hadn't gotten their primary work done on time, making the whole situation even creepier.

Lucretia's boss certainly doesn't take the time to give Elaine and Jim any special accolades. Although he does pat Elaine on the shoulder when he runs into her in the hallway and says, "Lucretia told me how great you were to help out with the special issues project. Thanks! You're fabulous." The next day he walks right by Elaine. He can't even remember her name.

Elaine and Jim are left feeling foolish, angry, and

exhausted. If Elaine had gone to Lucretia's boss on her own to explain her point of view, she might have gotten a demotion, passed over for a raise, or even fired. After all, the boss's job is to protect management, in this case Lucretia.

P.S. Lucretia is now the associate publisher of the magazine, even though she still cannot construct a sentence. Elaine and Jim are in exactly the same spot as they were before.

What Elaine and Jim should have done is thought of ways to expand their own jobs so that their boss could see and appreciate them. Shining for your boss does not necessarily involve a lot of hard work and long hours. Any extra work you do should only be done if you really want to, because it will help you get another job, or because you are sure it will have a direct, positive effect on your present job. Never assume or expect financial or title rewards from extra work. You will be rewarded for being able to handle yourself in front of important people, not for running yourself ragged.

You don't have to wear yourself out at work to get ahead. Do only what is required in your job, and you will climb the ladder faster because your load will be lighter.

It's Okay to Be Unprofessional As Long As You're Professional About It.

Let's look up the word *professional* in the dictionary. I used to be puzzled by the way that word is always slung about by people, especially people who seemed to me to be anything but. Anyway, here's what Merriam Webster's *Ninth New Collegiate Dictionary* says (abridged slightly): "a: of, relating to, or characteristic of a profession; c: characterized by or conforming to the technical or ethical standards of a profession."

Not very helpful, is it? Does your company have a definition of what their professional standards are? If they did, it would most likely be found in the company handbook. But I bet they don't. To most managers and executives, professionalism means not making waves. It also means figuring out who the important people are at the moment and being nice to them. It means different things for different people, depending on what their status is within the company.

It is very difficult to complain about someone who's being unprofessional, since most companies like to keep their definition vague so they can change it according to whim. I have found that if the boss says you're unprofessional, it just means he doesn't like you, or something you're doing annoys him. So, while Mary may be able to chew out John in the middle of the hallway, if Sally did the same, she'd be fired, even though they work for the same company in the same department. Get it? Mary is more important to the boss than Sally, so her professional behavior gets a lot more latitude than Sally's.

The whole matter of professionalism in the office is almost impossible to figure out. Let's say, for the sake of argument, that the definition of professionalism is to be polite and considerate of all your co-workers, regardless of status, to not gossip about company doings or employees, and to maintain a calm veneer under pressure. I bet you all agree. Ask any CEO, and he'd say yes. But once you left the room, he'd most likely double over in laughter. There are just too many people who disregard the rules of common decency and make wildly successful livings.

The question is, how and why do they get away with it?

Lets take Happi Thomas. Happi is always telling the people that she manages to be professional. By this she simply means don't complain, solve your problems yourself. She, on the other hand, is always crossing boundaries that she shouldn't. If she's not nosing into the personal lives of her people and her colleagues, she's saying outrageous things to people she harbors resentment toward. A lot, but not all, of her unprofessional behavior is on the personal level. For example, the assistant of one of her colleagues had a slight acne condition, but the girl was actually very beautiful, and you really didn't notice any flaw about her. Happi took it upon herself to buy some skin products for this girl and present them to her at her cubicle—out in the open—saying, "I understand how it is to have really bad skin. Try these products. They really worked for me." Of course, the girl was devastated and cried in her manager's office for half an hour. However, the girl's boss didn't say anything to Happi about this outrageous invasion of privacy, because that would have been unprofessional.

Happi once told Sally, "Always sit on the chair in front of my desk and not on the couch. I can't stand looking at your legs. You're just showing them off, anyway." She would not start the meeting with Sally until she moved. I would call this unprofessional, some might even call it sexual harassment, but Sally could never articulate this to anyone, first because it's embarrassing, and second, because it's the kind of behavior that's hard to pin down. Is it harassment? Is it rude? Is rudeness even against company policy? Probably not.

Happi's brand of unprofessionalism is just plain vicious, and the best way to deal with it is to ignore it and give her the pity she so rightly deserves. You should practice detachment in this kind of situation. If you don't respond, people will generally back down. Also, you can call them on it if the situation is right, and that usually works, too, depending on the person. The more you put up with a personal level of unprofessionalism, or **Jerkism,** the more you'll get it. This kind of bad behavior generally can't hurt you, but with a person as angry as Happi, you're still going to have to watch your back. And if you ever have to work for her, quit!

Then there are people who can indulge in behavior that actually borders on psychopathic, yet somehow they arrive at the top of the ladder untainted by their reputations. In fact, their reputations are often enhanced by their crazy streak.

I have a friend who works at a large furniture design company. Jane is the head of the sales department and Annie is the head of the marketing department. Annie doesn't like Jane, not for any particular reason, they just don't click. Annie is also very competitive. The boss likes Annie a lot. It's not that she's a genius at her job, but she does it well. Frankly, he also likes the way Annie combines looking sexy with a tough, truck driver mouth. One day, Jane was in Annie's office asking her about a particular product they were selling. She needed some marketing information and Annie became enraged at Jane's question, yelled, and threw the telephone at her. It missed by a long shot, but still . . .

Jane left Annie's office immediately. Everyone in the surrounding offices heard and saw what happened, and eventually Annie's and Jane's boss found out about it, too. Did he do anything? No. He did not reprimand Annie, and he said nothing to Jane by way of apology or consolation. *Nada.* Why? Well, as Jane explained it, "Chuck is not my friend. He likes Annie better." People will always be partial to one person over another; since most people aren't, in fact, professional, they will let that partiality stand in the way of their fairness and good judgment.

So much of success—and getting away with bad

behavior—is about making the boss think you're doing a great job and making him believe that any problems that arise are someone else's fault. I've never been nasty to anyone nor have I ever thrown anything at anyone. If I did, I'd be fired immediately. Why? Because there are people who have the flair to get away with outrageous behavior, and I'm not one of them. Annie's colleagues know the boss likes her, so they wouldn't dare complain to him about her. They know it would fall on deaf (and annoyed) ears; they would look like complainers, which is *so* unprofessional.

In the same design firm, in a different department, something else is going on. Matt has a hard time with one of his employees, Barb. They are always arguing, but Matt tries his best to work with this person because he has treated her very badly in the past and knows it wouldn't do to fire a person who has so much evidence against him. But one day Matt has had enough. He just can't take it anymore. Barb says something very nasty and hurtful to Matt, a reference to Matt's lack of education. This so enrages him that he slaps—yes actually *slaps*—Barb across the face. Then he fires her.

Matt goes to his boss right away and tells him the whole story. He's very upset. The boss is fond of

Matt and doesn't want anything to happen to him. In fact, the boss even tells Matt he understands why he would hit Barb. Barb wasn't really hurt, just shocked. Ultimately, the company had to pay quite a bit of money to Barb to keep her from going to court (she had a very good case, after all). But Matt was never reprimanded. The boss just suggested that he not hit his employees anymore, because it could get expensive. Indeed. Not too long after that, Matt got a plum promotion and a fat raise.

In creative businesses, like publishing, television, newspapers, movies, fashion, and design, bad behavior is tolerated more than in other kinds of businesses because creative people are thought to have fragile egos and the creative edge makes them more emotional and neurotic. It's the theory that artists are special, so their peccadilloes must be tolerated. This may be true, but it still depends on who you are, even in a creative shop.

Take Happi Thomas again. Happi is always butting in, making suggestions to other departments, and sending unnerving and embarrassing E-mails and notes to her colleagues. She enjoys intimidating those around her and has difficulty praising her people because she needs to feel superior to them. She goes out of her way to hire pretty young things, and by verbally putting them down, she gets enormous personal satisfaction and revenge for what she perceives as her own physical flaws. In other words, Happi can act out her pathologies in the office. Who needs to pay a psychiatrist $150 an hour when you have that kind of unchecked freedom?

When someone calls this behavior to her boss's attention, he may say something vague to Happi, like, "Be more tactful," or "You shouldn't put things like that in writing (it could get the company in trouble)." He never addresses the real issues of professionalism in the office, because frankly, he doesn't care. She does a perfectly good job, has been loyal, and it's too much trouble to hire someone new— possibly for more money—and break him or her in. He tells the complaining person, "Well, she can act that way because she's talented." The attitude that talented people can get away with outrageous behavior because they're endowed with some supernatural power is utterly ridiculous, but it will never change. The only thing you can do is figure out a way to live with that point of view. And just remember, talent is in the eye of the beholder (Truth #2).

In the first place, never take a position where a Happi Thomas tells you what to do, and if you're in one, get out. If you're stuck with one while you're looking for another job and if that person is being unprofessional to you, tell her in the most controlled, nonthreatening voice (Truth #1) you can. Never be afraid of someone so lacking in sensitivity and feeling. Her skin is made of leather—it may even look that way!

I once worked in a company that had weekly meetings about new ideas. The meeting was run by two people, and one of them always made faces whenever someone brought something up she didn't like, even before he had finished talking. She was a dreadful woman who had a superior attitude toward her colleagues because she considered her own social and economic situation to be better than those she worked with. These expressions were unflattering, so I'm surprised she made them so often. I have actually never been in a meeting in any other office where a senior person, a VP, would make faces—let alone while someone was still talking. It was disrespectful and unprofessional. However, she got away with it because no one ever told her to stop. You should be honest about someone's bad behavior if it distresses you. You should do it privately, so you won't embarrass the person (not that he or she would necessarily extend you the same courtesy). Suggest to the person succinctly and quietly (Truth # 1) that it might be better *for them* to stop whatever the behavior is. Often people will stop annoying behavior if asked, only because they are so surprised that someone noticed enough to speak to them about it, or if they think the change will be beneficial.

BEING NICE

Being nice has nothing to do with being professional. It also has nothing to do with being polite. People can be completely foul and still be polite. Being polite doesn't mean making everyone happy. Remember, there's only two people you have to keep happy. You and your boss. This is a disappointing fact of life, but one that you can figure out how to exploit.

Being friendly to everybody isn't going to get you anywhere. Someone was arguing with me about this once and pointed out as an example the former head of a very large publishing company who was reportedly mean, nasty, and uncaring to his employees (even the newspapers gave some lurid examples of this man's outrageous behavior). He thrived, however, as did his company, for many, many years. The importance of the bottom line almost always presides. Well, this guy got a new boss, and they clashed, so he was fired. Everybody said at the time, "Oh, so-and-so finally got what he deserved," and "He got his comeuppance!" Comeuppance?! The guy left the company a millionaire. Do you think next time he'll say, "Gee, I'll be nicer and more professional"? I doubt it.

I'm not recommending you start swearing at everyone in your office or put tacks on the chairs of your enemies (although it's tempting), but don't waste your time chatting everyone up and being perky. In fact, I think it helps to have a little edge. People aren't going to complain to your boss that you're not being sociable enough. Which *doesn't* mean you can't bow out of company functions—you have to go to at least a few of them, otherwise your boss will think you're not "a team player."

I know so many managers who belittle their people, ignore their colleagues, think only of their own agenda, and laugh openly at the notion of teamwork—and still flourish. They have the support of their bosses. And why, despite their despicable actions, do they have that support? For the five following reasons, in order of importance:

1. They never bring problems or complaints into their boss's office, except in rare instances. When

they do, they use a phrase like, "I have a con-cern . . ." instead of "I've got a problem . . ." For some reason, this simple choice of one word over another has a positive effect on the boss, even though he knows exactly what the person in front of him is really saying.

2. They are polite to their boss and other im-portant people.

3. They reassure their boss about the business frequently.

4. They have self-control when their boss is pres-ent.

5. They do their job well enough to maintain a standard that satisfies their boss.

Being professional means making sure your boss likes you and likes the job you're doing. That's it. End of story.

Be a Team Player—Just Make Sure You're on the Right Team.

I don't know when or why this concept got started, but I think it has something to do with a sports analogy; that is, football is no different from your office. The front end, the linebacker, the quarterback, can all be matched to a similar role in the office. I don't think so. In the first place, a sport or game is a finite activity with a time frame: a beginning, a middle (halftime, the cheerleaders), and an end. A company, on the other hand, does not really engage in any finite activities; there is no time frame in which an office operates; and there is certainly no set beginning, middle, and end, unless, of course, the company goes under, but that's unpredictable.

A team has a set number of players, with each player assigned a specific and clear duty. We all know that numbers of office workers fluctuate, and that most of us only have a general, not specific, idea of what we're supposed to be doing, regardless of job descriptions. A sports player's performance is easy to evaluate. His goals are defined, his technique is measurable. Unlike most middle managers, he knows exactly what he needs to do in order to win. It's much easier to define if a player did well or badly on the field. Judging performance in an office is just too blurry. So many other factors are at work; the members of your office team (or department) may help the other office team (or department) to your team's (department's) detriment. They'll be rewarded for being a traitor if the result is satisfactory to the boss. If a football player purposely helps the opposing team, they would be charged with throwing a game, and might be fined or suspended.

But the real reason the idea of the corporate team player is totally bogus is that in sports there is an effort to be fair. A game has rules to keep it that way, and those rules are clearly spelled out and known by all players. In boxing, opponents are equally matched: heavyweights don't play lightweights. In business, team players and opponents are rarely equally matched. Work *isn't* fair. It's not supposed to be. I don't care if the manager says, "Well, we need to be fair to everyone here, in this situation."

He's not going to be fair, because being fair to all his team players may not result in the outcome he needs. And he may not be making decisions based on his employees' abilities or on any logical criteria at all.

Team player is a manipulative idea conjured up to subordinate workers, to keep them in line, and to make them feel bad for being disagreeable. When a boss says, "Be a team player," he only means to say, "Do what I say and don't give me any back talk, and for heaven's sake, don't rock the boat, complain, or tell me anything negative about my employees, my company, or my product."

Managers will never stop using the term. It's great to use as an excuse for firing someone. "Jack just wasn't a team player; we had to let him go." In reality, Jack was probably pointing out a flaw in the system and the boss couldn't handle it. But firing someone for not being a team player can work well. It lets the human resources department know that Jack wasn't integrated into the office culture, and was considered distracting and destructive. A good, official reason for termination. Unofficially? "Get that annoying bastard out of my face!"

It's also a terrific way to avoid giving people promotions or exciting projects to work on. "Sharon, you've got to be a team player! We're all on the same team, working toward the same goal, so it doesn't really matter what you're doing," is the response Sharon gets when she feels she's ready to do a new, challenging task that the boss doesn't want to give her for reasons known only to him. Management uses the same reasoning when someone asks for a title change. "Jane, titles aren't important. It's what you're doing that really counts." If titles aren't important, then why is management so stingy about giving new ones out? Why do they only improve someone's title when a good person is on the verge of quitting?

The team player concept espoused by management idealizes all the things you shouldn't do in an office: share ideas, help out coworkers with projects, share important information indiscriminately for the altruistic good of the company, never check out the competition for your own benefit, and give credit to others all the time. If you do these things on a regular basis, you will become the rag that the team uses to wipe their cleats on.

The important thing is to learn both how to accept this stupidity (you're never going to change it), and to fake it as a team player (like all the successful people in your office do). Here are some important things you have to realize about being a team player.

To maintain a team player front requires some amount of covert activity that can, if you're not careful, lead to all kinds of bad behavior, like lying, backstabbing, and competition. Go team!

Here's a little something I read in a career column of a well-established women's magazine. It means well, but barely pays lip service to the reality that is the American office. "Make certain you're a team player," the magazine advises if you are preparing to ask for a raise. The article goes on to describe a team player as someone who fits in to the corporate culture, makes her values match the company's values, makes sure her work makes everyone else look good, never undercuts her peers, and is prepared to pick up the slack. Okay. Let's examine this and do a little reading between the lines.

As far as fitting into corporate culture goes, I agree. If everybody wears jeans to work, leave the Armani suit at home. If your company has political leanings that aren't yours, either get out or keep yours to yourself. But frankly, if you think pornography is demeaning to women, then why did you take the job at *Jugs* magazine in the first place? You get my meaning?

Fitting into corporate culture means making sure you don't clash. You have to look like everybody else on the outside, and every once in a while mouth some of the niceties and company slogans. That's fitting in. You can be yourself, do everything you need to do, and maintain your individuality and still fit in. Just be subtle about it.

Making everyone else look good? Don't go overboard. You know when the company has a party to celebrate some achievement, and the president comes in to give an inspirational pep talk and says, "We're a great team. Everyone worked toward making this a great year." Ask yourself: Am *I* going to get a better bonus at the end of the year? Am *I* going to get a promotion? Probably not. There are one or two people who will be rewarded, unless, of course, *you* were the one directly responsible for the job well done (and you made sure the boss knew it, which means taking credit for your own work, and *not* giving it to somebody else). The boss may talk about and praise team performance, but he rewards individuals.

Undercutting your colleagues? Well, I don't think it's a good idea, either, but I want you to count how many people in your office have successfully stabbed somebody in the back in the past year. Next.

Picking up the slack? You already know what that means. It means doing somebody else's work. I feel so strongly about this one, I wrote a chapter about it, it's Truth #6. *Read it again.*

Being a team player means trying to reason with unreasonable people. It simply cannot be done and will only drive you mad. Successful irrational people have used their unreasonableness for their own gain, so they have no plans to change. If you try to deal with them rationally, they will accuse you of a variety of things, such as being uptight, unwilling to be creative with the rules, and having a negative attitude. To be a top team player, you have to learn what approach will win over each individual in your office. One person may respond to charm, another to humor. Some people will like you to be direct and get out of their office quickly. In order to be a team player, you have to have sixteen personalities ready to go at all times to contend with all the other team players in your office.

A team player looks the other way when he knows something bad is happening to a colleague. During business hours, a team player swallows his integrity. He ignores colleagues who are rotten to each other, and will only blow the whistle on someone when he knows that person is unpopular and the boss will love anyone who can give him an excuse to get rid of him. Many people justify not pointing out someone else's bad behavior or rotten work by saying, "I can't say anything to the boss about John's harassment of his staff. I'm a team player."

People will tell you that a team player is someone who cooperates with his fellow workers to achieve the common goals of the company. This is utterly absurd. A manager, for example, is not a team player, but she needs all her subordinates to be team players for her. That way, she'll get all her work done, and they will never get ahead. The one who stops being a drone for the manager will be the one to get out of the grips of her boss and get a better job or a promotion.

Many stupid team players fare much better than their more sensitive or intelligent coworkers. "Well, Joe's not really that brilliant at his job, but he does whatever he's told, he's loyal, and he never gives me any trouble, so I'll support him until he retires. He's a team player. Plus, no one else will hire him." So, *team player* can become another term for a schmuck.

The real team player, the altruistic worker who's smart, sincere, friendly, cooperative, and hard-working, is usually thought of as not dynamic enough to be considered for a promotion. These people perform their jobs skillfully and quietly as middle managers until about age fifty-two, when they are laid off in corporate downsizing. Meanwhile, the Happi Thomases of the world are usually the ones who do the laying off: "Bob, you're really terrific, *really*. It's just that we don't need you anymore."

Fake team players know that they owe nothing to anyone who doesn't owe them anything.

Fake team players often profess collegial love. Happi Thomas, for example, is forever exclaiming, "Oh, I love Gabbi," when, in fact, she hates her. What business does someone who hardly knows you have using the word *love,* anyway? Yuck! Put these liars in the To Be Avoided file.

No work-related issue is ever solved until the person in charge wants it to be solved. No amount of team playing makes anything happen until the boss gives his okay. It has nothing to do with what the team wants or feels is for the best.

Take, for instance, those deluxe corporate retreats, seminars, and brainstorming sessions that occur every once in a while between senior and middle management and/or adversarial departments within a company. These costly therapy sessions make the bosses feel they've taken responsibility for the little people's well-being, to help them function better as a team. At these seminars, everyone sits around discussing ways to improve morale and to work together more harmoniously; then everyone goes out for margaritas. The next day, everything is exactly the way it's always been. Nothing has changed. The boss's approach to team playing is playing a few rounds of golf on the company tab and joking around with a few cute secretaries during the weekend retreat.

A colleague of mine told me how she and a couple of coworkers had met with their senior management to discuss ways they could be more involved with the decision-making process. These two senior officials tolerated them politely and even said they were enthusiastic about their ideas, and that they would put some of them to work. Plus, of course, how terrific it was to have had this marvelous interaction with them. Nothing changed until my friend got a better job offer. Then, all of a sudden, she became part of the decision-making process because they wanted to keep her. The moral: Teamwork does not apply to anyone who has seniority over you.

Indulge my digression here, and let me fill you in on a fun piece of trivia related to all this: Did you know that some kinds of teamwork may even be illegal in this country? Companies with nonunion workforces (88 percent of Americans are not members of unions) have two choices in terms of management style: They can dictate work rules and conditions of work with no employee input, or they can turn the operation completely over to the employees to run. Otherwise, they *have* to form a union. If they are found to be operating somewhere between these two options, like cooperating with workers and finding ways to improve conditions through a fair exchange of ideas, they risk violating section 8 (a) (2) of the National Labor Relations Act of 1935. I wouldn't necessarily bring this fact up next time your boss tells you to be a team player, but it's good for you to know that teamwork in the office is frowned upon by the laws that still govern this country. Still, many bosses like to have everything both ways so they're never cornered.

A while back, I read a very nasty article about Tina Brown, the editor of the venerable *New Yorker* magazine. I don't understand why people are always putting her down. Has she killed someone? This article described how she interacts with her employees, claiming that she talks to some people and seems to snub others. Then they write, "It's hard to imagine this [her behavior] being conducive to team spirit." If Tina Brown actually does this, at least everyone knows where they stand with her. She either sees you or she doesn't. She just probably has a lot on her mind and can't remember everyone's name. I'll take this any day over the boss who's always slobbering over the employees and telling them how great they are, how he loves them, then forgets it two seconds later. That kind of bullshit is worse for team spirit than Tina Brown's style because you really feel crummy when you discover the slobbering boss was insincere. You usually find this out when you ask for a raise or a promotion. All of a sudden, you're not as great as you seemed. Give me Tina Brown any day.

The only one who has to believe you're a team player is your boss. You don't have to worry about what anyone else thinks. That's the great thing about bosses: They only know one side of the story (yours, preferably), and they don't *want* to know the other side.

The bottom line is: When things get bad, who do you think will be the first to practice the every-man-for-himself philosophy? Mr. Boss, naturally. You know, the one who gave you the speech about teamwork when you were first hired?

Being a team player means getting noticed by the person who can help you the most. Playing the role of team player requires subtlety, finesse, and a strong stomach.

You Don't Need a Positive Attitude to Achieve Success.

"In Italy for thirty years under the Borgias, they had warfare, terror, murder, bloodshed. They produced Michelangelo, Leonardo da Vinci, and the Renaissance. In Switzerland, they had brotherly love, five hundred years of democracy and peace, and what did they produce? The cuckoo clock."

— Orson Welles, from *The Third Man*, 1949

"If only we'd stop trying to be happy we'd have a pretty good time."

— Edith Wharton

"A lot of what drives me is hate."

— Howard Stern

The whole idea that positive thinking will make you popular, rich, successful, and happy started with the publication of *The Power of Positive Thinking* by Norman Vincent Peale. While this book and the slew of imitations that followed proved to be best-sellers, they left many people feeling frustrated and depressed. Why? Because it's hard to force yourself to be happy if you are not so inclined. Positive thinking is such a readily accepted concept now that even to mention another point of view seems like heresy. But what the hell! I disagree. The solution to all your problems and the way to keep healthy is *not* just being happy.

The positive thinking mentality is quintessentially American. For some reason, our national psyche embraces the notion that positivity is the first and most important step on the road to eternal happiness and prosperity. If only we could wake up every day with a smile on our face, if only we could push every negative thought and pessimistic feeling out the window, we'd be 100 percent better off. Since this concept has no basis in reality, I can't really figure out why we're so enamored of it. It simply doesn't work for many people.

If you've ever been to Europe, you'll know that they don't have a problem with their negativity. Europeans walk around grumpy and discontented, and they're perfectly, gloriously happy about it. If you're waiting for a train in Italy, the workers invariably go on strike for five or ten minutes. But that job negativity gives them a little break, and they get back at their bosses. It doesn't seem to dampen anyone's spirits. Nobody goes home a failure because of it.

Have you ever heard a Frenchman say, "Just look at the world through rose-colored glasses and everything will be all right"? Of course not. They're content being suspicious, snobbish, and rude. All that negativity has served them well for a centuries. Of course, this *très charmant* grouchiness is balanced out by the fact that they get to go to the south of France every year where they run around naked on the beach and drink copious amounts of good red wine, something we don't get to do very often.

We, on the other hand, feel frustrated because we can't always be chipper and up, which in turn makes us think that we'll never get anywhere, which is self-fulfilling. I'm here to tell you that negative thoughts, along with positive feelings, are a permanent, natural state of the human condition, and that they can actually protect us from harmful people and events. I believe in **The Power of Negative Thinking**.

Drive, determination, will, and a strong sense of

self and purpose are what's really required for success—and these things don't necessarily have either a positive or negative quality. They have both. When I was editing this chapter for the final time, I came across an article in the February 1996 issue of *Elle* magazine. Amy Gross, editor at the time, interviewed Steven Turner, a tennis pro, about winning. I was thrilled when I read his comments about negative thinking. Someone had finally caught up to me about this issue. He said, "You have to bring the shadow out into the light—look it squarely in the eye. By confronting it you can harness its energy. Most people think energy is just in the yes. But it's also in the no. Once you tap into that negative energy, you're more whole. Then you can start to win." Finally! What a smart guy. And Amy Gross, too, for having the courage to bring his message to her readers.

I knew a manager who used to say about one of his employees, "Tom is so down, he's so negative, he'll never get anywhere." What the manager really meant was that he was *conscious* of Tom's negativity, and it bothered him. Tom made the mistake of not harnessing his negative thoughts properly. Big mistake. Meanwhile, there are several successful executives in the same office that are as negative and grouchy as they come.

The sales and marketing director of this company was particularly negative. You remember Clover Spite? Well, Clover has a big sign on her office wall that shows a picture of a hideous witch casting a terrible spell, and underneath it says, "Don't even think about talking to me until I've had my coffee." Of course, you could call this humor, but she's deadly serious about it. She also has a sign posted on the outside of her door, which is usually closed, that says, "The beatings will continue until morale improves—The Management." She finds this both amusing and useful as a half-serious message to her people. Her boss loves her. This kind of thing might not be tolerated—and neither would Clover—in another company. Clover knows this, which is why she'll never look elsewhere for a job. She knows a good thing when she sees it.

Clover has open disdain for her colleagues, whom she considers adversaries. She keeps her office door closed at all times, making it clear that she doesn't want to be bothered, and in general, she walks around looking pretty disagreeable. However, Clover doesn't tell her boss what she thinks of her colleagues, so she's never really thought of as negative. When she does criticize people in front of her boss, it's couched in a way that makes it seem like she just wants to do her job better, that somehow her victim is hindering her progress. The boss knows exactly what Clover is really saying, but her method makes it a lot easier to deal with.

In fact, her negative attributes help her achieve status in the company. People are afraid of her and don't like being around her, so they pretty much do what she tells them to do. Plus, nobody wants to go in her office because she smokes like a fiend, and it stinks in there.

Clover's boss is well aware of her perceived negative style, but she says, "Clover knows what she is. I like that!" What does she mean by that? That she's blue collar, rough around the edges, and isn't it great that she uses it to her advantage? Yes. Just the way royalty used to think court jesters were fun to have around or in the way that wealthy people think poor people are noble savages, the boss thinks Clover's style is quite charming and amusing—and she gets the job done and keeps costs down. Mainly by handing out stingy raises.

If you're by nature a negative person—or a serious person or a cynic or a pessimist—you're wasting valuable time struggling to change yourself. *Love who you are*. Instead of studying ten books on how to be positive, you could be figuring out how to get your next promotion or a raise or a better job.

Positive thinkers usually can't bring themselves to be ruthless enough to protect their turf and do the work that's required for success. Although your closet negative office mates will praise you for your happy attitude, they'll be dumping work on you and moving ahead in line at the same time.

A few negative attributes, like slight paranoia or a natural distrust of others, can make you more sensitive and aware of people who may hurt you. You can also use your negative feelings about yourself to great advantage. Look at Happi Thomas. She's always telling her staff to be positive, to bounce right back after something bad happens. This is the way Happi gets them out of her office when they come to her with an issue or concern. She makes them feel guilty that their problems are merely the result of their own negative attitudes.

However, Happi's success is built on a solid foundation of negative thinking and negative attributes. It's what gets her out of bed every morning. Happi wakes up and looks at herself in the mirror. She can't believe she's thirty pounds overweight, and she hates herself for it. She looks at her skin and realizes that even with the silicone injections, it still doesn't look youthful and smooth. She can't do anything with her hair, either.

She goes down to breakfast and has an argument with her husband. Why can't she please him? Why does he always put her down? Why is he always mad at her? It must be her fault.

By the time she's out the door, dressed to conceal her upper thighs, foundation and rouge covering her bumpy face, promising herself to be better to her husband, her self-esteem is in pretty rough shape. The thing is, she has incorporated this negativity into her very being. It's part of her. She gets to work and looks at all the pretty young energetic things in her department (who she hired) and they depress her even more.

These negative thoughts and feelings propel her forward. She pushes the sweet young things to accomplish as much as they can (making her feel superior to them even though they are more attractive than she is—something that torments her). She'll be goddamned if any of her problems are going to hold her back. She's ruthless with colleagues, steps over them, and crosses social boundaries. She gets what she wants.

There is tremendous energy contained in negative thinking, possibly even more than in positive thinking. Instead of fighting that energy, you can harness it to your will to a positive effect. That's where the difference lies: Instead of letting your negative thinking keep you from accomplishment, use it to press forward! No more guilt!

Now, I'm not saying that if you are by nature a happy person with a positive outlook on life that you should try to become negative. What I'm saying is that all humans feel negative at times, and trying to fight it only causes stress. *All* your feelings and emotions can be used to your advantage, even the negative ones. So enjoy them!

There is no proof that the bad vibes of one person can do anything harmful in an office. It just doesn't work that way. If it did, there would be thousands of people and companies who would be all washed up, and they're not. I would bet that more successful businesses have been and are run by cynical, negative people than by positive ones. Why? Because they anticipate problems more readily, and they generally have a plan. They find it easier to get rid of useless or unproductive people, and they are less prone to be taken advantage of. And they certainly don't waste any time being nice.

We have driven the idea of cause and effect to the precipice of insanity. For example, I was working in a particularly odious office a while back and someone was giving me the royal screw. One of my superiors actually told me that my bad mood was "dragging the company down." I'd like to mention that the company's profits were then at an all-time high. The people in the office couldn't have cared less about my mood or the fact that a colleague was screwing me. My negative attitude just made this superior feel guilty about his own ineffectuality in handling the situation. *That's* what he was so upset about.

After the Civil War, the country's economic and industrial success was built on the backs of a bunch of curmudgeonly, pessimistic, grouchy capitalists—the robber barons—including Rockefeller, Morgan, Vanderbilt, Carnegie, Harriman, Gould, and Frick. Do you think they were spending their spare time writing inspirational speeches about looking on the bright side and feeling happy? Do you think they even considered for a moment that if they were happier, they'd be more productive? Did they sign up for evening classes in developing self-esteem and positive thinking? No way. They let their negative views influence a nation and build great wealth for themselves.

Here's a list of some successful people, past and present, who have learned to harness their "negative" qualities—overly analytical, pessimistic, critical, fatalistic, sarcastic—to great advantage. So next time somebody tells you to stop being so negative, reread this chapter and look at this list. Then go back to your desk with all the negative energy you can muster, and succeed!

Stanley Crouch (rhymes with grouch)
H. L. Mencken
Tallulah Bankhead
Philip Johnson
George Bernard Shaw
Pauline Kael
W. Somerset Maugham
Gertrude Stein
Truman Capote
Woody Allen
Kenneth Tynan
Carrie Fisher
Linda Ellerbee
Orson Welles
Roseanne
Norman Perelman
Donna Shalala

Oscar Wilde
Dorothy Parker
Ethel Barrymore
James Thurber
Norman Mailer
Saul Bellow
Abraham Lincoln
Alfred Hitchcock
Fran Lebowitz
Jacqueline Susann
Ezra Pound
Bette Davis
P. J. O'Rourke
Jimmy Breslin
Eldridge Cleaver
Jilly Cooper
Richard Snyder
Howard Stern

If you accept your negative nature, it will work for you, not against you. And, by the way, donate all those books you bought about acquiring a positive attitude to a prison.

It's Okay to Use People as Long as You Don't Throw Them Out When You're Through.

*T*he word *use* seems like such an ugly, selfish word, doesn't it? It conjures up images of opportunists, con men, schemers, and turncoats. My definition of the word is on the other end of the spectrum. I could have called this chapter "Networking," "Learning the Big Schmooze," "Socializing Your Way to Success," or "Flirting for Fulfillment," but they just didn't sound right. And not one of them would have captured your attention as dramatically as the one I chose.

There used to be a system of mentoring in companies that rarely exists today. You would be taken under the wing of a superior and he would carefully nurture your skills, enabling you to rise through the ranks. This hardly ever happens anymore. Our country has developed an every-man-for-himself attitude that fosters selfishness and doesn't allow for the generosity that mentoring implies. Second, holding down a job is hard enough right now, so your boss may be thinking, "Why should I train you to take my place at a cheaper rate, when there's no guarantee that I'll be promoted, too?" It just doesn't make economic sense. There's also the question of loyalty. A company used to invest in someone for the long haul because there would be mutual allegiance involved. Unfortunately, there's not a lot of that going on at present.

So, in lieu of finding a mentor, you have to use a variety of people for different reasons. But you have to be smart about it. The first thing you need to do is figure out what you want. You need to create an agenda for yourself. If everybody in your office is running around with an agenda (and they are) and you don't have one, you'll just become unintentionally swept up in somebody else's. Not a good thing. To use people effectively, you must be completely confident about your agenda and be willing to do the work necessary to achieve its expectations.

Once you've set your agenda, all your actions and decision making should support your goals. Remember that you will not achieve everything on your list right away, so prioritize what's most important.

For example, it may be important for you to change bosses before you start. You should concentrate all your efforts on finding people who can help you get reassigned or on finding a new job entirely.

Learn not to be afraid of what you want. David, for example, has his eye on eventually becoming the head of the research department of the pharmaceutical company where he works—or, in fact, the head of the research department of any other pharmaceutical company. However, while he's smart enough, he doesn't have the self-confidence required to make this happen. His fear of the goal itself causes all kinds of problems. He's afraid of asking for help; he's afraid of taking important risks; he's afraid of people saying no; he's afraid of failing the first or second time out. He's scared that people will laugh at him or turn away from him.

George, on the other hand, is focused on the same goal. He's not afraid of what he wants, he has a clear vision and knows that this job is very important to him, so he is not apprehensive about doing all the things he needs to do to secure it. He doesn't care if someone says no to him; the next person may say yes. He's not afraid to take action, to introduce new ideas, to risk sounding like a fool. He's not afraid to ask people in his department, other departments, and other companies for help and advice. He's taken the time to figure out who the best people are to go to for the things he wants.

Guess who's the head of research now?

FOUR QUALITIES TO BRING TO THE PEOPLE YOU HAVE CHOSEN TO USE

1. Know what you're talking about

You must learn as much as you can about the subject, so you know it inside out. When you go to someone for help, they'll have confidence in you because you'll know the right questions to ask.

2. Respect and thank the people helping you, and reciprocate if you can

I guess this seems pretty obvious. But you can't imagine how many people there are who help someone out and never get thanked. There are some people who completely ignore people who have helped them once the deed is done. It's as if they think acknowledging someone else will tarnish their accomplishments. It doesn't. Please don't be a person like that. And if you help someone and she doesn't acknowledge your efforts, never help her again. It's also unnecessary to thank someone who's never done anything for you, just to be nice.

3. Follow through

If someone gives you the name of someone to call, call the person. If someone goes out of his way to send your résumé to a company, contact the company. Don't let opportunities slip through your fingers by not taking each one to its conclusion. Maintaining your contacts is very important. Don't let a relationship die because you're too lazy to return a phone call or write a letter or note. *Consistency* is key.

4. Don't be afraid

Here it is again: fear. Don't be afraid to ask for help or advice. Don't be afraid to introduce yourself to people. Don't be afraid of not getting what you want the first time out. It will come eventually, and in the best way possible, if you want it and you're doing all the right things to get it. Take the word *fear* out of your personal dictionary.

USING YOUR BOSS

If your boss seems willing to let you grow, stick with him. Many bosses are notorious for holding people back for as long as possible, until they are forced to give a promotion. If you have a boss like that, and you can tell pretty quickly if you do, get out as soon as possible. This is a clear sign of a boss's insecurity and unsupportiveness, two things you want to keep as far away from as possible.

If your boss is one of the rare few who is willing to see you grow and develop, you must do a lot of work yourself. You cannot expect your boss to remember every wonderful accomplishment you've made over the course of a year. That's why you must keep track of what you do (Truth #3) so that when review time comes, you can make a good case for yourself. Don't be passive. It also doesn't hurt to regularly, subtly remind your boss of your talent, efficiency, and skills. One way of doing this is to never complain. Remember Sylvia with the six mink coats? If you don't complain, your boss will think you must be an extraordinary human being. Come up with additional responsibilities—especially ones that aren't too labor- or time-intensive—that way you'll be quietly building your power base and demonstrating your competence.

Assess your boss's strengths and weaknesses. Determine what he knows the most and least about. Then focus on filling in his weaknesses and become knowledgeable about the things he's least familiar with. This will be much more effective than trying to do all the things your boss is good at and competing with his knowledge of a subject. Once you've put yourself on this path, your boss will become more user-friendly when you want a raise, advice, or a professional favor.

Using Your Colleagues and Coworkers

There are many people in the office who can make your life easier. Go out of your way to be nice to the subordinates in different departments so that later you can count on those people to go the extra mile for you. This is simply common sense. They will respond to your kindness, because they're used to people treating them as if they were invisible.

Colleagues have information you need, know people you want to meet, and can teach you skills. Find out who has what, and seize the moment. Just be prepared to pay them back in kind. If Tim is going to spend time teaching you the new profit and loss program on your computer, you better be willing to reciprocate. For example, with a tip about a new job he may want or a favor that can help him meet a deadline. Of course, there are people you should never accept anything from, because they'll never let you forget it. For example, a woman I once worked with brought me back a souvenir stuffed animal from a vacation she took. I accepted it graciously and thanked her. Some time later, she was trying to tell me how much she had done for me (she had done nothing except bring me grief), and screamed, "I even bought you a present!" Oh, brother! Whatever some people are offering usually isn't worth the aggravation and manipulation it will bring. Once you've figured out who these people are, avoid them, and gracefully decline their offerings.

USING OUTSIDE PEOPLE

Often, people from outside companies will be more willing to help you than they are the people in their own company. Why? Because it's less of a threat to them. If they help someone in their own universe, that person may surpass them at work. An outside person is less of a risk. It's human nature.

The other great thing about having good contacts with the people in your industry is that if your company sees that you are known and respected by outsiders, they'll think of you as more valuable, and they'll try harder to keep you happy. It's the old dating theory. You're always more popular when you're going steady than when you're looking around.

You should be meeting new people who can enrich your knowledge and enlarge your professional scope. If you have an expense account, use it and any other perks as often as you can. Taking people out to lunch who are in a position to help you is extremely important. There's nothing wrong with asking someone to lunch or for a drink because you want to get to know him. But don't ask someone for a job the minute you meet him. You can only force bulbs, you can't force friendships.

I have a rule of thumb whenever I go to any party: Meet three new people. As much as I'd like to, I don't hang around only with the people I know. This may not always lead to your most enjoyable evening, but it's worth the effort. It reinforces your confidence and gives voice to your goals. If you're shy, or if you feel too tired to make the effort, then go to a function with a friend and meet new people together. I have a best friend that I do this with, and it works like magic. When we're together, we feel stronger and more energetic.

Remember, meeting people, using people, whatever you want to call it, should be fun. Don't make it a desperate mission. People will see the frantic nature of your attempts and be turned off.

Ask someone for a favor, but make sure you're deserving of it.

The Office Is Like a Garden: Weed It.

*T*his doesn't mean you should fire everyone you don't like, because you're probably not in a position to do that. What I do mean is to cut down the time you spend with people who don't do you any good. Evaluate what you need from the various people in the office, and figure out how to get it.

There's talking and there's talking. Exchanging polite pleasantries and getting what you need are different from shooting the breeze about the weekend with someone you despise just because you think you have to. You don't.

You don't have to deal with creeps if you think of yourself as *The Victory Garden's* late Jim Crockett. He knew how to stop a nasty weed or thin out a patch of wild **Morning Glories** (better known as **Choke Weed**).

Make a list of all the people that really, really bother you at work, and next to that write down why, with a few icky things about them to make you feel better. Don't worry, you don't have to show it to anyone. There's no sense wasting time trying to look on the bright side in search of wonderful qualities in people that aren't good for you. By writing these outrageous things down, you can exorcise the feelings you have about these people and get them out of your life. It will help you understand that the individuals who bother you at work are not all-powerful monsters.

By looking at the specific behaviors that bother you about someone, you can figure out how to manage that person out of your career and get on with things. Plus, sometimes it's fun to be **Healthy Negative.**

For example, here's Sally's list:

Person	Why	Icky
Happi Thomas	Passive-aggressive, insulting, tries to sabotage me "sweetly"	Fat, bad skin, terrible dye job, husband calls her names in front of colleagues
Joe Schmuck	Can't make decisions, lies, changes mind all the time, Inconsistent manager	Humorless, no taste, boring, can't ride a bike
Gabbi Boucher	Steals ideas, talks over everyone, gossips, manipulative	tasteless clothes, face looks like one of those dolls made from an apple

Okay, now you have to admit, you feel a little better just reading that. I hope you giggled a little; I know I did. What's really important is that Sally has narrowed down on paper the list of people she really needs help dealing with. Just remember: Read this paper when you're feeling a little bit depressed about work and keep it at home.

Now, if you wrote down every person in your office, or if you wrote down people *under* you, get another job right away, or visit a psychiatrist. You should never have hostility toward your underlings, unless they're **Eve Harrington**. If you hate everyone in your office, there's a real chance you have a complex of some kind that I'm not trained to identify. Get help!

On average, there are probably three or four people at work who annoy the hell out of you and could possibly do some damage to your career. They are most likely at the same level or one step above you.

I bet when you looked over Sally's list, you recognized all those people. You might even think Sally works in your office and she's writing about your colleagues. You know them because they are common office types. They *are* in your office. They are **Office Diseases (ODs)**.

Gardens cannot thrive with disease, and neither can you. Let's see how to get rid of this blight. Take Happi Thomas. As we know, Happi is a very sad woman. She is also angry and frustrated. Sad, angry, unattractive, and frustrated people are very dangerous to be around. If liquefied, those four things could create an explosion stronger than the most powerful hydrogen bomb.

Luckily, Sally does not report to Happi, but Happi is responsible for whatever goes on the cover of the magazine, including the headlines that announce the stories and features, so Sally does find herself at Happi's mercy on occasion. Happi is one level above Sally and isn't her boss and has no real control over her day-to-day activities, but she does have decision-making power over something important to Sally. This is a typical dynamic in every company. There's always someone who's sort of your boss.

Sally cannot go to her supervisor about Happi because Margaret is at the same level as Happi, and she's not going to do anything about it. Besides, Margaret hates Happi even more than Sally does, and she's managed to cut her out of her life. Margaret is certainly not going to bring her back in for Sally! Also, and this is important, Sally knows it's very unwise to complain about Happi. Happi has been with the company a long time, and complaining about her would look very bad (even though Sally knows no one likes Happi, and there are many legitimate complaints against her—as she's heard from Gabbi).

What does Sally do? She prunes her contact with

Happi. She takes the advice of one of her colleagues, who tells her that she deals with Happi by ignoring her. In meetings, she is silent when Happi makes a comment and quickly moves to the next thing. She disregards Happi's memos, and only goes so far as to say hello when confronted with Happi. So, while she can't "control" Happi's behavior, she can maneuver it so it has minimal effect on her.

Sally does not engage Happi in conversation, because she knows it will make her feel raped, manipulated, and insulted. She does not pay attention to Happi's suggestions about her own work, and she does not respond when Happi makes a comment in a meeting. She doesn't have to. Sally has analyzed the situation and realizes she needs only one thing from Happi: to get an occasional tag line on the magazine cover. *Nothing else.*

Sally has learned never to contact Happi directly (even though it would be considered appropriate in this setting). Instead, she goes through Margaret, her boss. She chooses carefully what tag lines are important to her and pitches Margaret passionately. Once in a while, there is something she needs to fight for without Margaret, so she visits John, her equal in Happi's department, and deals with him. Sally devises all kinds of Happi detours, and most of the time

it works. In fact, lately, Sally has been getting a record number of tag lines on the cover of the magazine.
Sally has a mantra that she repeats at least once during the day: Get it done without Happi.

The times when she fails to get a tag line, she
shrugs her shoulders and moves on. This is called
Weeding out what is important and what's not important. She just doesn't care if all her tag lines don't
get on the cover of the magazine. At least Sally's husband loves her and doesn't insult her in front of other
people. (This is why it's important to fill in the Icky
column of your list—it acts as a reality check.) Listen, if one of twelve plants dies in your garden, do
you have a nervous breakdown? No, you pull it out,
throw it in the compost heap, and use it for mulch.
Same thing with Happi.

What does Sally do about Joe Schmuck? Every
company has a Joe in a decision-making position
who can't make decisions. He gets other people to
make them. Then he says (and thinks) that he made
the decision himself. Sound familiar? Of course it
does. Someone like Joe is probably sitting a few
doors down from you.

How come an idiot like that is a VP? Because
every company needs a decision maker who can't
make a decision. When the boss makes a decision for

Joe, who claims it as his own, and it doesn't work, the boss has an instant scapegoat. That's certainly worth a couple of hundred thousand a year, don't you think? Also, every boss needs at least one manager to dump on.

Even really smart, talented people at the top, people who are really good at their jobs, hire incompetents. These wimps will never be a threat to their position, and will always do what they are told. For a boss, it's nice to have a few of these types around.

Now that you know why there are always going to be Joes (of both sexes) around, let's get down to dealing with them. Just remember: Joe is scared, insecure, unhappy, and hates himself. The only thing you need from Joe is a decision. So forget about his miserable psyche. Avoid him (like you avoid Happi) and make the decision yourself. Just make sure he thinks it was his idea.

Write a multiple choice memo. Present Joe with the necessary answer or set of answers. Ask him to say yes or no, or to choose one. Joe will run to his boss when you're not looking, the boss will make the decision, and then Joe will give you his carefully considered reply. Yes! It's generally that easy! Just make sure you have a written record of it, and thank him for his timely attention to the matter. No sweat!

Gabbi is a tough one. Gabbi is usually hard, cynical, and mean. She considers her superiors as beneath her because she naturally feels better than they (and she may well be). She also holds strongly to the idea that she is a good person and is above any kind of reproach. There are two things not to like about Gabbi: her face. *Do not,* under any circumstances, tell Gabbi anything personal about yourself, your job, or your frustrations about work. Because eventually, Gabbi will use that information against you.

Remember, Gabbi is the person who cultivates her superiors' assistants to get information out of them. She's always luring them into her office for lunch from the fanciest Italian deli in town. Then she gets the dope on their bosses with her way of seeming like a concerned mentor. When she's away on vacation or business, she even lets the assistants use her office for private phone calls and lunches. So all the twenty-four-year-old underlings think she's supportive and kind, and because of that, Gabbi knows what's in all the VPs confidential interoffice envelopes. Talk about knowing how to use people!

Since Gabbi can't help herself, she will probably tell you as much as she can about everyone in the office. She loves talking and being the Grand Central Station of information. But keep whatever she tells you to yourself. Figure out how to use it later, discreetly. Never gossip yourself (see Truth #4). If you are polite and avoid her most of the time, you'll do fine. Knowing Gabbi's strange hyper-moral, hyper-uptight view of the world, she'll probably tolerate you. Keep it that way.

If **Eve Harrington** is your assistant, fire her immediately. If you can't fire her, give her lots of work to keep her busy and miserable. Don't be nice to her, reveal anything personal, or help her in any way with her career. Don't give her the keys to your desk, your PIN voice mail number, or the code to your computer. Because, believe me, she'll be in your office on Saturday making note of your Thursday dinner date and God knows what else.

Be professional, cool, hard, precise, and stay away from nice-nice chitchat. Don't ask her how her weekend was. It also helps to wear heels (if you're a woman!) so that you're *always* taller than she is. **Eve Harrington** is a Gabbi Boucher, Happi Thomas, or Clover Spite in the making. If you do all of the above, she'll realize you're too much trouble to stab in the back, and she'll eventually go somewhere else if you don't can her first.

If your boss is impossible, try to get reassigned. If that's not in the cards, do what he/she tells you to do, keep notes, modulate your voice, flatter only when absolutely necessary, be courteous, and get away from him or her as soon as possible. If your boss lies to you, tries to cheat you out of something, or is abusive, and you have been keeping records as you should be, you can confront your boss with confidence and get what you want. You won't be fired for being right if you play the professional-modulation game, especially if you have evidence. We'll refer to it here as **Fertilization for Future Growth.**

Being a good **Office Gardener** means avoiding personal contact with dangerous people (the gossips, the insecure, the unhappy, the ugly, the threatened) and eliminating from your daily activities the ones that you can. Trying to make friends with them or search for their positive qualities will only fail or backfire. Use them only for what they're good for. Don't ask, tell them what you want. Your office garden will be lush, green, and mite free. Congratulations! Now you have a green thumb!

The final **Weeding** process is to get another job. If you've done everything in this book, and you still feel your work environment is unbearable, start looking for something else. All offices are not for everyone. Even very successful businesses can have very,

very sick offices, and they usually thrive on that sickness. Some people like the anxiety and anger that a dysfunctional office creates. They feel comfy there because it's familiar to them, probably a reminder of home. It may not be for you, and that's a good thing. Besides, changing jobs is sometimes the only way to meet a new challenge, get a really big promotion, or make more money.

Evaluate what you need from the people in your office, get it, and stop there. Do not overfertilize.

We Love You! You're Fired!

Part of surviving successfully in the office is handling yourself and your career well when you lose your job—for whatever reason. Statistical employment reports say that on average, people will be fired, laid off, or their job will be eliminated or made redundant three times in their career. That's an average; for some it will be less, for others, more. No matter how good, talented, hardworking, skillful, and creative you are, you can still get the shaft. After all, business is business.

What do you do if you are fired? Cry? Call your mother? Tell your boss exactly what you think of him? For a lot of people getting fired is a lot like death. They just don't want to think about it until the time comes. This is not cool. Start thinking about it now. Work yourself through the whole scenario in your head. Predict how you will feel. Who will you seek advice from? What kind of severance will you ask for?

Some time ago, I was watching an Oprah show about people who had fought back successfully against crime. Many of them were people who were mugged or robbed. Oprah's expert guest was a private detective, and he gave the audience a very important tip. He said that the greatest advantage that a criminal has over his victim is surprise: he has a strategy, and you don't. The mugger certainly doesn't have an economic or intellectual edge, but he's got premeditation on his side, so he can overwhelm you. This PI suggested that you work out ahead of time what you would do if someone came up from behind you and stole your wallet. The same kind of premeditation gives management an advantage over you, and they know it. I don't see any difference between a mugger stealing your billfold and your manager asking you into his office one Friday morning to tell you not to come in on Monday.

The element of surprise is often the biggest thing the person who's doing the firing has going for him. When you're surprised, your reaction time can be slowed down, and you are put into the shock mode; this gives management even more time to have things their way, which will not be beneficial to you. But if you have a plan, you can contain your emotions, respond quickly, and focus clearly on the issues of your termination, because you know what your response to management will be. Another bonus is that management will be astonished at your preparation, and that will catch *them* off guard.

Of course, even with a plan, you will still be initially surprised. Really bad news, like really good news, is always hard to believe at first. But knowing what you'll do beforehand will shorten the shock time. Important spiritual leaders tell us to live each day as if it were our last. I agree. That philosophy should be carried over into the workplace. Assume every workday is your final one.

Most employers can fire you for just about anything they want, with a couple of exceptions. There's an 1884 Tennessee Supreme Court decision that states, "Men must be left without interference to . . . discharge or retain employees at will for good cause or for no cause, or even for bad cause, without thereby being guilty of an unlawful act." While most states adhere to this principle, there have been some laws passed to protect workers from being fired without cause. Some are pretty specific. You can't be fired for serving in the military, going to a political convention, or serving on a jury. Of course, any kind of firing based on discrimination, whether it is because you're African-American, female, Jewish, Chinese, gay, short, or over fifty, is also strictly forbidden. But there are other laws that are nebulous and are of particular importance here. They are firings that violate good faith and fair dealing.

As of this writing, there are a few states that do not have these kinds of restrictions. They are Delaware, Florida, Georgia, Louisiana, and Mississippi. But if you work in those states, that should not deter you from seeking a fair and reasonable settlement if you have been fired for no cause. There's always a way, and that way is usually found in a good lawyer's office.

Let's get back to *fair dealing* and *good faith*. These terms can work to your benefit if you've been fired for no cause or if you've been laid off. The object of the game is not so much to keep your job (Do you really want to work for someone who doesn't want you?) but to secure your future for some amount of time and to get help in finding another job. There are no guarantees that even the best severance package in the world will actually get you another job, but it certainly increases your chances and allows for a better comfort zone than an unemployment check.

The good thing for employees and the bad thing for employers is that the terms *fair dealing* and *fair play* are vague. They can be broadly interpreted to build a case for getting a better settlement. These can include breach of promise. Did your boss constantly tell you that you were a star and that you were important to the company, or that you had a strong future with the company before he fired you? If the answer is yes, then he has lied to you, and this can be put in the category of unfair dealing and breach of promise. How about telling you you're going to get promoted and you're not? How about telling you your work is excellent, then two months later telling you it's bad and firing you? Think about the reasons he's firing you. Does appearance, gender, age, or disability come into play? Or, is it because it's easier than solving the *real* problems in his office?

What's your plan? Part of it should be to have a list of people who you can call immediately to ask for advice and/or assistance regarding new work. Call them as soon as you can after being dismissed. You should understand and make note of what your value is in dollar terms (pay plus benefits plus pen-

sion plus 401K). This will help when you are negotiating severance. The following are other things you
should either have on hand or anticipate doing when
you are fired. They will help you be **Fired Smart.**
Most are useful in negotiating the best package possible:

To Be Fired Smart . . .

Get your papers in order

The memos, documents, notes, and reviews that
you have been keeping will enable you to reconstruct
a pretty accurate picture of your employment history
with the company and the events leading up to the
firing. A lawyer, if you decide to hire one, will need
this information to represent you well.

**Obtain a copy of your company's employee
handbook**

This item usually outlines, among other things,
the policy regarding termination. Most handbooks
have a disclaimer that states that they can change
their minds about the policy any time, and that it has
no legal bearing—they can and it doesn't—but it's

handy, and basically spells out a company's philosophy regarding the treatment of employees.

List the contents of your personnel or Human Resources file

Do this as soon after you've been given notice as possible. Actually, you might want to see it and make the list beforehand, if you sense trouble. This file is yours to see at any time, no questions asked. This is important because some companies are notorious for sticking bogus notes with false dates into files claiming that they warned the employee or attempted rehabilitation or they make note of professional weaknesses. If this kind of behavior doesn't make you think twice about teamwork, I don't know what will.

Ask for the reasons for your dismissal in writing

Write down your version of the events of your firing while they are still fresh in your mind. Compare the official reasons with the real reasons. Is there a difference? If there is—and most likely there will be—it may help your case if it goes into dispute.

Consider your future job prospects and write them down

How difficult will it be for you to get another job in your field? How much income will you lose if you don't get another job for two to five years (increase your salary about 5 percent per year, which is an average salary increase, to estimate this). Has your reputation been tarnished? Will you have to seek employment in another field? Will you have to take a job at a lower salary?

Face your accuser

Never negotiate with a human resources drone. Not that the people in those departments are bad, they're just useless because they're getting their orders from somebody else. They're not cutting a deal with you themselves. Also, confronting your manager, if you can do it, gives you enormous psychological leverage. He's going to be uncomfortable, no matter how he may present himself. Since you're prepared, this gives you some strength. Also, he's the one you're bargaining with, so you're going straight to the source. Get the terms of your termination in writing. Remember, this is just a first offer, no matter how adamant he is about saying that it's final. It's going to be the minimum, and it will be laughable.

Some employment professionals say that unless you're a top executive, the most severance you can expect is a couple of weeks. It's true that the more important you are and the more money you make, the larger your severance will be. However, if you're in any kind of middle or senior management, or equivalent, and you're fired for no cause or for suspicious reasons, I feel you can and should try to get more than what management is offering. You have to try. But you better have good reason, and you better be prepared. Severance negotiations are neither fun nor easy, but they can be interesting if you can keep yourself detached emotionally. And they are an exercise in perseverance, tenacity, and will.

Agree on your termination announcement

What do you want the company memo to say about your departure? Write out your own, then ask to read the company's version to see how it compares. It will be easier to make changes to their version if you've thought about it beforehand.

If the company wants you to leave immediately, get them to provide professional outplacement service

You may also be able to get its "cash value" added to your settlement if you don't want to participate in the service. Many lawyers negotiate outplacement service, which is worth a lot of money (between $5,000-$10,000), as cash because outplacement gets mixed reviews from people. I've talked to people who consider outplacement a factor in their survival. Others think it's a joke. It depends on the career counselor and the placement firm you are working with.

You should also find out if you can be placed in another part of your company. Transferred, if you will. Sometimes, companies do this anyway, sending you to Siberia in hopes that you'll quit. Actually, this isn't such a bad thing, because you're working and getting a paycheck while you look for another job, so I wouldn't write it off immediately.

Request a written reference before you go
Make sure you have the signed reference in your hands before you pack and ship your last box home.

Think hard about whether you want to retain a lawyer

This is a big decision, because it is costly and time-consuming. Be prepared. A good lawyer will make you do a lot of legwork before he or she takes your case. But a good lawyer will be a tremendous comfort and help to you during this trying time; legal counsel is worth its weight in gold and more.

Bringing a lawyer into the picture can have one of two effects. It can make your employer a bit easier to deal with or it can make the company mad. That's why your case should be worthy if you decide to consult a lawyer. Either way, your employer will be incredulous that you would bring in legal counsel. I can't explain why someone who has just turned your life upside down would perceive you as being disloyal because you've sought counsel, but there it is. The lawyer is on your side, and you need someone who's on your side and can do something about the situation.

How to find a good lawyer? Get a referral from someone who was happy with their settlement. A legal firm that has worked with your company before is preferable. They will know the ins and outs of the

place, and they'll probably know the company's lawyers, too, so it can be a lot easier. Ask your friends.
Nine times out of ten, they will know another friend
who went through the same thing and can give you
a referral. If you can't get a referral, then you're going to have to call reputable firms and take a chance.
Go to the library and look up recent newspaper ac-
counts of local employment suits—if the outcome
was employee-favorable, call the law firm mentioned
in the article. Meet with a lawyer first (it will most
likely cost you money), and if you don't like him,
don't work with him. You've got to feel comfortable
with your lawyer. If you do your homework, you
should be able to get a good contact. In fact, you
should have a name of a lawyer in your Rolodex at
all times.

Lawyers work in a variety of ways. Some employees choose not to speak to their ex-employers
from the point of being fired onward. The lawyer
does all the talking for them. Some lawyers will advise you, and you'll do the face-to-face negotiations.
Many will do a combination of both.

If you simply can't come to an agreement, and
you really feel you're right, that you're being screwed
for a heinous reason, then you have to consider either

compromising or suing. I recommend compromise, unless a lawyer feels you have a strong, winnable case. Most employment lawyers would rather do their jobs from their office, not in the courtroom, so be prepared. Lawsuits are serious business. They are expensive, time-consuming, psychologically draining, and very public. Once it's in court, it's everybody's business. That's something to think about.

CONTRACTS

Some companies will ask you to sign a contract when you begin working for them. Some middle managers think it's a status symbol to have a contract, but there can be a downside unless you are in the upper echelons of management. A contract is as much, if not more, for the company's protection as it is for yours. A contract provides you with some amount of security, but if you're terminated, you have just as much leverage, and maybe more, if you don't have one. The negotiation is so much more open and creative if there isn't a preordained agreement sitting in front of you. So don't be glum if your company doesn't offer you a contract. Remember, they only give tenure at college.

GOOD-BYE

The final termination agreement should be fair to all parties; it should offer you security for a period of time that is commensurate with your years of service, not on your performance for the last six months; and it should extend you some assistance in finding other work. Expect confidentiality to be part of your settlement, too, which is something you should take seriously and respect once the understanding has been made official. The settlement should bring you some peace of mind and some resolution and closure to the ordeal of being terminated. You shouldn't feel angry after you've gotten a fair settlement, although up until the time you do have one, your anger should keep your fighting momentum up if the bargaining drags out. *Make your anger work for you.*

Once everything is resolved, your job search will loom in front of you like a dark, endless corridor. But you have to start walking. There are a million books available about looking for work, so I'm not going to start on that here. Basically, finding another job means hours of mailing letters and résumés; making follow-up phone calls; feeling frustrated, lonely, and rejected; becoming resentful when you have to take your pajamas off and get dressed to go across the street to buy the want ads; and sometimes drinking more vodka than is really necessary. Don't forget about all those people you met after reading Truth #10. Eventually, you will find another job, or you'll start your own business. That is where faith comes in, something you must practice daily to maintain.

When you get fired, you are no longer on the same team, so have your plays worked out early in the game.

Glossary of Terms

Bitter Bob or Betty: A person who blames outside circumstances for his or her self-loathing.

Bloodsucker: A person who initially seems nice, but whose only interest is in getting you to do things to better his or her career. Insecure, unhappy, frustrated, and selfish people.

Commendation: Any oral or written note of praise, in either an official or casual format.

Eve or Evan Harrington: A character from the film *All About Eve* who will do everything and anything in her power to get ahead. In an office, Eve can be male or female.

Fired Smart: Doing all the right things when you get fired to come out as unscathed as possible (and preferably with a check in your hands).

Fertilization for Future Growth: Any activity that ensures your job security.

Healthy Negative: Owning up to your negative feelings about people and situations without guilt and without letting those feelings permeate your day.

Hurricane Harry or Hanna: A person who cannot be pinned down or counted upon to be fair or consistent.

Jerkism: The practice of being a jerk.

Judgmental Judy or Jack: A person who is impossibly stern and rigid. Someone whose expectations you can never live up to (nor should you want to).

Missing Vertebra: See **Jerkism**.

Morning Glories/Choke Weeds: People who will take over your life if you let them.

Office Disease (OD): A person at work to be avoided for numerous reasons.

Office Gardener: A person who knows how to rid his or her life of useless, dangerous, destructive people.

Pathological Monster: A nut you should avoid.

The Power of Negative Thinking: Harnessing your negative thoughts and feelings about yourself, others, and the office into energy that will propel you forward to success. The knowledge that a bad attitude can be very useful.

Selective Gossip: The art of choosing what gossip to spread and what gossip to keep to yourself.

Unofficial Information: Information that you obtain about a person or company that has no specific bearing on your job but may help you understand a colleague better or protect you from someone manipulative.

Weeding: Getting rid of anyone or anything that hinders your movement forward in the office.

Karen Randall is a writer and editor who has survived countless office jobs. She lives in New York and Pennsylvania with her husband and two cats.